the *jonathon*
letters

One family's use of support

as they took in,

and fell in love with,

a troubled child

by Michael Trout and Lori Thomas

ISBN 0-9761546-0-9

Copyright© 2005

The Infant-Parent Institute, Inc.
328 North Neil Street
Champaign, Illinois 61820

contents

preface

Perhaps you have to know Lindsay, in order to fully understand what it was like to be beckoned into service by this particular cousin. She is a special-education teacher, and a good one. She also coaches kids' sports, and generally devotes her life to being in the presence of children who are having a rough go of it.

But I know lots of people like that, and they cannot get me to do things that require me to dig so deep. Lindsay can, and she did, on a particularly beautiful winter morning, a couple of days after Christmas, in the year 2000. Happenstance put us at breakfast together in a grand, windowed restaurant in northern Virginia that morning, and I liked everyone at the table: my wife (with whom I was enjoying a few rare days away from our kids, who were all visiting other family members), my beloved uncle Doug (Lindsay's father), and this little-girl-who-can't-possibly-be-a-grownup-much-less-a-complete-professional cousin of mine—the one with the tender eyes and the freckles.

She knew a family. (Oh, Lord, already I'm in trouble. It's Christmastime, and we have to talk shop.) Their adopted, Korean son was in her special-education class, and she adored him. She also admired his family, and had become quite close to them, which was why it caught her attention when she discovered they were thinking about taking in another deeply troubled four-year-old boy. They were foster parents, but they had a habit of adopting the children who crossed their threshold, and it was going to be tough, with this one.

Of course, I could not be expected to take on a clinical case, at this distance (my practice, thankfully, was far away, in Illinois, while the family lived in Virginia). But would I be willing to let them write me—just once, she assured me—about what they were seeing, and maybe I could answer a question or two for them?

Lindsay knew that word had gotten around, over the past couple of decades, that I knew a bit about attachment problems in early life, and what happens in foster and adoptive families who take on a child whose early life has been marked by abuse, neglect, multiple losses, domestic violence, and that curious, sometimes intergenerationally-transmitted, sometimes adaptive absence of empathy that results in children becoming particularly lost, desperate, angry and almost as determined to never attach as they are starving for attachment. I receive calls from all over the country, from parents absolutely at the end of their ropes, and the stories resemble each other: "He seemed so sweet. They didn't tell us about the abuse, or even about the four disrupted placements that preceded the one at our house. We thought we could love him out of it. When the behavior started, we were so thrown off by the suddenness of its emergence that we were sure it was an aberration. After all, others [at church, sometimes even at school or pre-school] see him as so angelic. So we thought, at first, that it was our imagination that he had this wicked look on his face when he stepped on the puppy's face, as he walked across the room [or when he "accidentally" made the baby cry, or when the fish tank was mysteriously knocked over, or when things started disappearing from my drawers, or when I noticed the odor of urine coming from his closet, or when I awoke at 2AM to find him standing next to my bed, with a knife in his hand]. Help us! What can we do? We don't want to send him back, but he is destroying our family!"

Typically, I listen, commiserate briefly, sometimes offer to send a little packet of journal articles I keep in my files for just these purposes, ask about the family's local resources, and then move to the punch line: "I'm sure you understand that I cannot help much further than this. You need, and deserve, high-quality clinical and developmental support in order to make this placement work, and in order for your family to survive. [I happen to think that this is the absolute least we owe foster and adoptive families, when we ask them to commit their hearts and their checkbooks—while putting at risk their marriages, their other children, their privacy—to endeavors of this magnitude.] I certainly can't give you this, from the other side of the country (or even from one or two states away). I am so sorry."

Lindsay understood, of course. It was wholly impractical. And there were professional ethics to consider. But she kept staring at me. (What a presence she is. No wonder children with such limited internal resources give their all for her.)

Of course, you know what happened next, else this book would not be cradled in your hands at this very moment. I caved. With limits, of course. One letter from them. No promises. If they asked a question I could answer, or if I could suggest a reading or other resource, I would give it one try. That's it.

Perhaps Lindsay knew that I would find this family as compelling as she did, and it would not end with one letter. Or, perhaps, she thought that something was better than nothing (and she may have known that, for many foster or adoptive families, those are, indeed, the choices: a little something, or nothing). So we made our deal (I don't remember if I got hugged, but I probably did feel like a hot-shot for about two minutes), and a breakfast that would change my life for the next year was concluded with (by comparison, at least) small talk.

A few days later, the first letter arrived. You will soon see why I was captured, why I could not bail, why I gave so much energy to looking after a family on a mission.

The collection of letters you are about to read is largely unedited. They do not represent a clinical intervention; that was not the contract I had with this family. While I was explicit about the nature of our agreement and the definition of what we were doing, I did not have a plan for how it should unfold. I didn't know if long-distance support was even possible. What would it mean to become so involved with a family I had never met? I had clear notions about what sort of developmental guidance and support families needed, in situations like this. But I had only delivered such support in the context of extensive knowledge about the family, bolstered by my seeing changing affects as the stories unfolded and new information was integrated.

In this non-clinical relationship, would I be more forthcoming about myself than I usually am? Would I acknowledge that I was raising a step-son with serious attachment problems, arising from his adoption at age 7

months (following a life of nine months inside a mom who had relin-
quished seven previous children to adoption, and who knew, unequivo-
cally, that she would do the same with Jeremy, and then another seven
months of his lying, unstimulated and unloved, in a Guatemalan foster
home)?

Did I become friends with Lori? Certainly, I sat in awe as I watched the
story of their family's struggle unfold. Certainly, there was a growing intimacy, as we chatted—sometimes late at night or very early in the morning, before my first patient arrived and before her home exploded into the
cacophony of everyday life—about the most important matters of her life
and soul. But what was the name for this particular brand of exchange:
one that is, by definition, unbalanced, one that is out of the ordinary, one
that is probably time-limited, even as both participants are beginning to
realize that the connection will, in some form or another, last a lifetime?

Our hope is that these letters will be meaningful to you. If you are a parent, we hope they will support you as you fight through your own
ambivalence and your child's extreme resistance to find a way that you
can survive, and your child can get what she needs. If you are a professional, we hope these letters will encourage you to stay with a family who
is at risk of being torn apart by the multiple, exasperating, seemingly-
inconsistent needs and constantly-changing behavior of a child who has
seen pain few of us can imagine—and who offers not the slightest grati-
tude to a family that earnestly wants to make it all better for him. We
hope you find, in Lori's forthright answers to my repeated questions
about what made her stick to it—what in her past, what in her marriage,
what in her heart, what in her faith—something that is meaningful to
your own battle to figure out the answers to the same questions. Lori
taught me that there really are some identifiable characteristics of families
who are likely able to go the distance with attachment-disordered children. It is not a job for everyone. It is not about being "good" enough to
handle such children. It is about having the resources—external and
internal—that will allow you to do things that are just not natural. I don't
know that I have those resources, but Lori and Paul did.

Michael Trout
Urbana, Illinois
January, 2004

introduction

Reactive Attachment Disorder of Infancy or Early Childhood first found its place in our diagnostic and classification manuals in the 1980's. The wave of children from Romania and other Eastern bloc countries startled well-intentioned adoptive families all over America in that decade with their astounding listlessness, resistance to affection, and developmental delays (Federici, 2000).

But they also brought something else that we had seen before: an enormous rage, mixed with an absence of empathy and a tendency to hurt little creatures. These features had been seen in particularly traumatized American foster and adoptive children, but we had no diagnostic nomenclature, or even a sense of the symptom clusters, the etiology or how to approach treatment. Foster and adoptive families recognized the similarities, as did a small number of clinicians. Establishing that there was a constellation of symptoms, and a particular etiology, helped us to see what was wrong with the institutional children from far away. These same clinical advances helped us to better understand certain of the traumatized and abused or neglected children who had earlier confounded us, right here in America.

Marcy Axness suggests a modification of the nomenclature, from RAD (Reactive Attachment Disorder) to NORMAL: *Natural Organismic Response to Massive Abandonment or Loss* (Axness, 1999). I prefer her term, not only because it is descriptive, but also because it suggests that this is one of those disorders that *makes sense.* In other words, once we understand what has happened to a child who later stands by our bed at 2:00 in the morning, with a butcher knife in his hand and a cherubic look on his face, or who methodically kills the kitten, or who does everything possible to make us hate him—while being amazingly charming to people outside the family—it all begins to make sense. It is, indeed, a *natural, organismic response to massive abandonment or loss.*

Children who present with behavior and affect that suggests they fall on the RAD continuum, then, have nearly always experienced a profound level of chronic neglect, physical and/or sexual abuse, some kind of separation from—or loss of—the primary attachment figure (if there ever was one) and, most often, an additional element: some sort of trauma, mixed with the abuse or neglect or loss. The trauma can be a one-time event (watching mom shake another baby in the family to death), a systematic pattern (repeated beatings and torture, or denial of human touch and stimulation) or it can actually be created by the system designed to "save" the child from such treatment: repeated placement disruptions and loss of primary care.

Clinically, such children do not present uniformly. Some are withdrawn and inhibited. Some are indiscriminately sociable. Many are highly intelligent, and often manipulative, while others are listless and uninvested in either people or inanimate objects. Some display delayed bone age or other signs of poor physical or mental development, while others are of normal stature and may even be precocious in one or another area of development. Some are overtly cruel, and will deny culpability even when caught red-handed. Others are more sly. Some are immensely charming, while others lack even basic social skills. Some experience extreme anxiety, with consequent problems in focusing and concentration and a tendency toward nightmares, while others display a startling absence of anxiety, even in stressful circumstances. But most share some of the following characteristics, to one degree or another:

1. deficits in the capacity for giving or receiving affection;
2. self-destructiveness, ranging from self-biting, to pulling out hair in clumps, to putting themselves repeatedly in harm's way (running into traffic, going anywhere with strangers);
3. deficits in the capacity to experience empathy for others, manifestations ranging from cruelty to animals or babies, to chronic blitheness about the pain of others;
4. a tendency to steal, hoard or gorge on food (and sometimes non-food items);

5. a tendency toward chronic, undifferentiated lying;
6. unusual patterns of eye contact, frequently characterized by gaze aversion;
7. a high level of interest in fire, blood, and gore;
8. a smoldering rage.

There has been little agreement about treatment. After years of being insulted by our inadequate referrals to ill-trained clinicians in local mental health centers, foster and adoptive parents began revolting a decade or so ago, demanding that we take their descriptions of home life with these children seriously, and give them some help. Many found reason for hope in the various holding therapies, ranging from the modest approach of Margaret Welch (Welch, 1988) to the more controversial methods taught and practiced by Foster Cline–and the many practitioners and revisionaries that followed him, and established the therapeutic communities of Evergreen, Colorado (Cline, 1990; Cline, 1992; Keck and Kupecky, 1995; Levy, and Orlans, 1998; Magid and McKelvey, 1987; Thomas, 1997). Although it became clear to most clinicians who worked regularly with these children (and, most assuredly, to their depleted and exasperated foster and adoptive families) that traditional "talk therapies" did not work to produce behavior change in these children—much less shifts in their apparently damaged characters—some were uncomfortable with the holding therapies, and worried about re-traumatizing already-damaged children. There seemed, however, to be something important about the containment that these "radical" therapies employed. Holding therapists began to emphasize cradling rather than control, and there were proposals for other treatments that did not employ holding at all (James, 1994), or that used elements of a the new, less-intrusive holding therapy with strong parental guidance (Hughes, 1997; Hughes, 1998). Modified forms of treatment strategies earlier developed for other populations emerged (Jernberg, 1979). A national organization, ATTACh, now serves as a gathering place for practitioners and foster and adoptive parents to pool their experience and talent.

But what is this thing, what does it do to the children, and what happens in the families with whom they live?

From the observations of "war babies" in Europe in the early 1940's made by Anna Freud and Dorothy Burlingham (Freud and Burlingham, 1943), to the proposals for an entirely new way of thinking about how the growth of love bonds may be hampered by the hurts of the parent's past suggested by Selma Fraiberg at the University of Michigan (Fraiberg, Adelson and Shapiro, 1975), attachment was studied with increasing vigor in the last half of the last century. We knew that children required certain reliable social experiences to develop optimally (Bowlby, 1951; Provence and Lipton, 1962; Rutter, 1970; Spitz, 1945; Winnicott, 1975; Yarrow, 1967), and we eventually came to understand that babies play a substantial part in eliciting attachment behavior from a parent (Brazleton and Cramer, 1990; Hrdy, 1999; Lozoff, et al, 1977; Stern, 1985; Trout, 1982). We were astonished to learn of the mental life of babies, particularly how adaptable they seemed to be, and how active they were in developing internal working models of the world—and their part in it—that would help them anticipate what was to come (Beebe and Lachmann, 1994; Bretherton, 1987; Main, et al, 1985; Stern, 1995). We were not fully prepared, however, to grasp the extent to which early experience would reside in the baby for years to come. And we may not have appreciated that the brains of infants and toddlers actually change, as they ramp up their vigilance in response to early trauma, for example, or as they interpret new experience only in the light of previous experience. ("My last three foster parents sent me away. This foster parent will send me away. It would be very stupid of me to make myself soft and vulnerable and available to this foster parent, because it will not last. Only a dumb organism would fail to get prepared for the inevitable: another placement disruption, another loss.")

It now appears clear that children who display signs of RAD have delayed or even damaged function in primitive areas of the brain (Schore, 2001; Schore, 2002; Siegel, 1995; Siegel, 1999). They do not respond to didactic or talk therapies because the areas of deficiency are in the largely nonverbal areas of the right orbitofrontal cortex and the amygdala (Schore, 2001). They do not plan their behavior (difficult to believe, sometimes, when one takes note of the devilish look in their eyes, after they have just urinated on the pile of clothes in the closet, or punched the kitty), and they cannot explain their behavior. They do not, typically, acknowledge being in pain (except when such pretended affect can be used to temporarily improve their position, or get them something they want). They can appear quite sophisticated, which makes it difficult to continue imaging them as extraordinarily small, helpless, primitive beings. They cope very well with stress, oddly enough; many have been raised in environments in which "…their little bodies are…subjected to huge amounts of stress hormones and endorphins. Their bodies basically 'learn' to expect…high levels of these chemicals…In later life, they often engage in behaviors designed to stimulate their bodies to produce high levels of these chemicals. Thus, they often do dangerous things, and seem not to feel appropriate levels of pain in response to what would be painful stimulation for anyone else. They often only feel alive when they have high levels of these chemicals present in their blood." (Randolph, 1995, p. 2).

For parents of such children, the challenges are enormous, if not overwhelming. They are often unprepared by the child welfare system that placed the children with them in the first place. They are often under the impression that love will take care of everything. Indeed, many fall into serious self-doubt and even depression when this prophecy fails to come true (White, 1997). It seems upside-down, to say the least, that the child's behavior may become worse over time; indeed, many foster or adoptive parents report that the child's resistance to affection becomes greater in direct proportion to the amount the parent gives.

One mother offers her perspective:

> *Within 24 hours of getting her, I was sure that I had made a terrible mistake. Two weeks earlier, when I saw her for the first time, my first thought had been, "Don't do this, Dianne." But she was only 6 years old, and there had to be hope for a 6 year old child.*

> *Little did I know I was about to become educated about attachment disorder, and how living with it can turn an intelligent, reasonably articulate adult into a complete basket case in a matter of weeks.*

> *Within the first hour of the adoption, she was pulling things out of the glove compartment and throwing them out the car window as we were driving down the freeway. My animals wouldn't go near her after the first day. While tucking her into bed that night, she reached up as if to give me a hug. Then she pulled my hair as hard as she could and said, "Sorry Mom, it was an accident." That was just the beginning of [her] spending every waking minute looking for ways to hurt me or anyone else…*

She tried to poke a baby's eyes out, hurt my animals,...said she wanted to shoot me in the heart with a gun, called my nephew and told him she was going to break his arms, molested other children and adults, grabbed two school principals' genitals, masturbated in public, lied constantly about the most obvious things, destroyed her room and everything in it, went into screaming rages when she didn't get her way, would look at you with this defiant smirk on her face while she stood there and wet her pants or put food all over herself from head to toe, and felt no remorse about anything...

No adoptive parents should be made to feel that the problems these kids brought with them are their [the parents'] fault. And no normal parents should be expected to just automatically know what to do to help these kids. Normal parenting doesn't work with them. There is nothing normal about attachment disorder. It is an insidious condition that can ruin the lives, relationships, futures, families and health of everyone involved if it isn't treated properly...

Adoptive families, with love and compassion in their hearts, unsuspectingly take in children who have never bonded, thinking they can make up for the love the children missed—only to discover that the child is incapable of giving or accepting love, and only feels extreme rage inside which translates into violent behavior. These families are being physically threatened and abused by the children they are tying to help. Many family members develop post traumatic stress symptoms from living with these rage-filled children. Unless that rage is treated and released, it will continue to grow, and all members of society will pay the price. To let the child continue with that internal turmoil, and the families continue in crisis, is abusive. (Allred, 1993, pp. 1-2).

This book makes no pretense about solving the problem of disordered, conflicted, disorganized, or otherwise inadequate attachments in the lives of babies and toddlers. Nor does it offer a formula for adoptive and foster families staying fully refreshed and alive in the face of stupefying challenges from children who seem to have no limits—either to their emotional needs, or to their capacity to wreak havoc inside the apparent safety of a family.

Instead, what you will find herein is an accounting of one family's experience: their early naivete (soon replaced by startling bolts of reality), their march into treatment, their ambivalent but somehow inexorable movement toward adoption, and their use of very long-distance clinical and developmental guidance from someone (MT) whom they had never met, who did not know Jonathon, and who had little to offer except an understanding of the diagnosis and a willingness to listen.

If I had to condense into two lessons all that I learned from being a faithful observer and supporter of this family, it would be these:

> 1. NO FAMILY CAN DO THIS ALONE. A combination of high-quality treatment and ever-ready developmental guidance and support are the absolute bare-minimum requirements for a family to survive life with a child with an attachment disorder—much less to be instrumental in his development into a child with the capacity for human connection. They also need friends, faith, permeable boundaries in their personal and family life, a sense of mission, a reason to put everything aside each day, and resources inside the soul of the marriage that allow it to sustain blow after blow. We cannot ask families to take on this mission—on behalf of all of us, really—without being willing to meet these bare minimum requirements for sustenance. This book—while not being held out as a model for the provision of developmental guidance at the family's beck and call—does, at least, give us a glimpse of what such guidance can look like, and how it was used by one family.

> 2. Foster and adoptive care for a child with an attachment disorder is not for every family. It is not even for every foster or adoptive family. There may be identifiable characteristics of families who do have the internal and external resources to go the distance. It behooves us to figure this out, as a society, as child welfare experts responsible for making and supporting placements, and as foster or adoptive families thinking about whether they are a match for the next child brought to their doorstep. I asked Lori repeatedly about what it was, *exactly,* about her family that allowed them to survive, and for Jonathon to flourish in their midst. Lori offers some insights; they deserve careful reading, on the off chance that they might improve the lot of another desperate child, and equally desperate family, somewhere.

chapter I.

How We Got Into This Situation
Lori Thomas, Jonathon's Mom

I just tucked Jonathon into bed. He gave me a hug and, with his sweetest smile, told me he loves me. My heart leaps when he says that. Tonight, I reflect back on the moment I first learned about Jonathon.

That day in November 2000 changed our lives forever. Our social worker called, and said she had a child that she would like us to consider adopting. He had a sad history, with several placements and a failed adoption. Would we please consider taking him into our home and family?
We met with the social worker and looked over his file. What we saw was a mess. Violence. Anger. Frustrated families. So much destruction, and the poor child was only four.

In our hearts we wanted to help him. We really did. But we had five other children to consider, including one with special needs. We absolutely could not accept this child. It would be unwise, and unfair to the others. We struggled with the decision. We said no.

A few weeks later, the social worker called again. They had found an adoptive home for the child, but needed a place for him to stay, temporarily. The adoptive home was not quite ready, but it looked like he would be able to move into that home in about four weeks. Could we consider taking this child in for just four weeks?

We can do just about anything for four weeks. Why not? We looked at the file again, saw the beautiful smiling face, and said yes. For four weeks we could take in this child. We would be happy to love him and care for him, temporarily.

So it was that on one bitterly cold afternoon in January, we met Jonathon. We loaded all of his belongings into our car. Our newest foster child came home.

"Our family has just taken in a new foster son. His name is Jonathon, he is four years old, and this is his fourth home."

This was not an heroic beginning to our journey. We did not bravely encounter the road ahead. We just agreed to parent a child for a few weeks. What could be so difficult about that?

As you read our story, I want you to keep that in mind. We agreed to a short-term placement. If we could have seen the road ahead, I am not sure we would have taken it.

That road, not taken, would have been the wrong path for all of us.

I hope you enjoy our journey.

Lori Thomas
Herndon, Virginia

chapter II.

From the Therapist's Perspective
Jon Barlow, L.C.S.W.

I first met Lori by telephone. She heard about the "attachment work" (see Hughes, 1997; Hughes, 1998; Levy and Orlans) I do, and wanted me to meet with her, her husband, and their new foster child. He had been diagnosed with Reactive Attachment Disorder, and they were hoping that I might be of help.

I had one concern about the situation. The family had no long-term commitment to the child, so attachment work would be more difficult. In spite of this concern, I set up an appointment, committing—if they were willing to do the work on their end—that I would do all I could as their therapist.

At our first meeting, Jonathon was completely unable to engage. He looked away, and his lips were in constant motion. He made a little sucking noise, like a kitten that was weaned too early. He could not stand to be touched, and fought any kind of holding with all of his might. It appeared that these behaviors were deeply entrenched. He was not going to let anyone get too close to him. It was evident that Jonathon had let his guard down one too many times, and been deeply injured. At this point in his life, it appeared that he had made a decision to keep control. No one would be allowed to tear down the walls of protection that he had built around himself.

Based on the story of his life passed on to me by Lori and Paul, and my own observations of Jonathon, all of this made sense to me. I had to understand these enormous defenses as functionally adaptive—even sensible—while disagreeing with Jonathon's contention that he could only be safe if he were alone. So I began to move in, gently but insistently. He lay on Lori's lap, on my couch, physically supported but not seriously constrained by her. I began to talk with him about what he had experienced, about his fear of vulnerability, about how smart I thought he had been to look after himself this way—while slowly raising the possibility that he might be mistaken in imagining that he would always be left, that he would always be injured, that there was no hope.

Jonathon avoided eye contact with me and, of course, with Lori. He scowled. He raged. He threw his body about, as if my words (or was it Lori's gentle touch?) were tortuously oppressive to him. It was clear: Jonathon exhibited the classic signs of Reactive Attachment Disorder.

We began therapy sessions weekly, but it was soon clear that we would need a more intensive effort, and shifted to a twice-weekly routine. Paul and Lori were willing to learn how to parent a child with RAD—an often counterintuitive way to love and look after a child—and to continue the work on a daily basis in their home. Jonathon fought them at every turn. The work—both in my office and at home—produced tremendous discomfort for him. I was asking him to give vulnerability a try and that was, by his accounting, a very stupid idea. Sometimes, as he raged, he would put words to his fears: "Why did my other mommies give me away?" Mostly, however, he resisted verbal engagement, fought touch, sucked on his bottom lip, and maintained that amazing scowl.

An oddity in this process was that Paul and Lori had established, a month or so before we began therapy, email communication with a therapist in Illinois who was knowledgeable about attachment and its disorders. Evidently, this man was willing to offer some long-distance support to the family, as they began their journey of discovering, parenting, and falling in love with this child. Throughout the therapy, they continued their email correspondence, and it turned out to be a helpful adjunct.

This unusual supportive structure—with one therapist available locally and another available at a moment's notice by email—seemed to work, for this family.

In the pages ahead you will read of an incredible journey. There were trials and triumphs. It was wonderful to be a part of it all.

Jon Barlow, L.C.S.W.
Healthy Steps, LLC
Burke, Virginia

chapter III.

The Letters: The Early Months

*"If emotions were allowed to
rule us, I would be completely
insane by now." (Lori)*

January 26, 2001 (the very first email)

Dear Mike,

Hello. I am Lori Thomas, mom of James, who is one of Lindsay's
students. Lindsay is more than a teacher to us. She is family, and I do not
know what we would do without her. James and Lindsay have an incredible bond, and we all love her. That, however, is not why I am writing to
you.

Our family has just taken in a new foster son, Jonathon. He has a
clear attachment disorder, and is very defiant. He will be five years old in
June, and this is his fourth home. He was with birth mom and assorted
family members for the first two-and-a-half years of his life. He then was
given up for adoption, and was placed in a foster home. He remained
there for nine months. He was then placed in an adoptive home, and that
adoption disrupted. He was with that family for ten months.

I met the adoptive mom, and have nothing good to say about her. She
appears to be a very cold, controlling person. She previously adopted a
baby from India, and that child is now two. Her bond with her quiet
little girl is clear. She does not understand why it was so hard to take in a
3-1/2-year-old (Jonathon), and bond with him. Jonathon is busy and
loud. He is taking Adderall for diagnosed ADHD. She wanted a passive
child, and wanted him to learn to play violin. She placed him in a
Catholic Child Development Center for full-time childcare. The reports

5

from that school show (to me) that the school staff developed a clear dislike for Jonathon. Rather than reporting his activities objectively, they used words like, "He delights in tormenting the other children." I do not think this poor little boy was accepted by anyone in his last placement. They all wanted him to be someone else.

The reports from his previous foster family show a very busy, sometimes defiant little guy. The extreme aggression that was reported in his adoptive home was not seen in his previous foster placement. We have not seen it here, either. What we do see is a confused child who really wants to control his environment. (He needs to control something in his life.) He does not obey if it does not please him.

Jonathon met us last Wednesday at an agency. He was brought there by his adoptive mom. After a short visit, my husband (Paul) and the adoptive mom went downstairs to move Jonathon's belongings from her car to ours. Jonathon looked at me and asked, "Where did Dad go? I thought I was getting a dad!" No mention of the mom, who also left. When they returned, he hugged Paul. He asked me, a bit later, what he should call me. I told him he had choices. He could call me Mrs. Thomas, or Miss Lori. When he wanted to, he could call me Mom. He said, "OK, Mom, let's go home."

Jonathon loves to hug, and wants to be held often. Of course, I am happy to accommodate. He has told me three times that he knows that when he is bad, we will send him away. He refers to himself as stupid and bad. I have told him that he is wonderful, smart and good. I told him that all of us have bad things we do sometimes, but that does not make us bad. Those are just mistakes, and we learn from them.

Yesterday I had to run out for a short errand, and left Jonathon with Rebecca, my 16-year-old. He was fine with me leaving but, when I came back, he ran up the stairs, hugged me, and said, "Mom! I knew you would come back!" I wanted to cry.

Jonathon's future is uncertain. There was a family lined up to adopt him, and he was to stay here for a month or two while they settled into their new home. They seem to have changed their mind, and have not met Jonathon. He is welcome to stay here as long as necessary, but we have mixed feelings about proceeding to adopt him, ourselves. ("Mixed" means that I want to, and Paul is concerned.) We have five children, and are in the process of adopting a sibling group. We have not met them yet, and do not know for certain that this will take place. Our current permanent children are:

Joshua, age 19
Rebecca, age 16
Patrick, age 13
Maggie, age 10
James, age 8

Maggie and James are adopted from Korea. The others are birth children. James has special needs, and is a very wonderful little boy. He was adopted at the age of 18 months, and has far exceeded doctors' predictions. He is a loving, sweet, busy boy. Maggie was adopted at almost seven years of age. She is terrific. There was a difficult transition with her, which we expected. She is now doing great, and we have all bonded very well.

None of our experiences have prepared us for Jonathon. We really need advice. We want to help him but have not been able to commit to him as his forever family. What can we do, at this point, without making promises to him that we cannot keep?

Any ideas? I really think Jonathon will be here for a while, and want to do all I can for him. Any advice you can give will be greatly appreciated.

Thank you so much,
Lori

January 27, 2001

Dear Lori,

You certainly hit the nail on the head when you say you understand that Jonathon's controlling manner results from his having been able to control so little in his years. You seem to be asking:

1. whether his behavior with you right now is predictive of what his behavior is going to be in coming months and years;
2. whether there is something insidious in him that might emerge later;
3. whether you should be as thrilled as you are when he seems to be showing signs of attachment to you;
4. whether the disrupted placements hide secrets about Jonathon

(or is it about the families, you must be wondering?!) that
explain why he doesn't stay anywhere permanently.

I doubt that you need me to tell you that those are all legitimate con-
cerns. The answers to all of your questions lie hidden in the answers (not
all of which are accessible to us) to these additional questions:

1. What was his prenatal life like? (Was there domestic violence?
   Did his mom think of aborting him? Did she have predictions
   about the baby inside of her? Did she drink, use drugs, smoke,
   rage, eat properly, get prenatal care? Was she depressed? Did she
   want him?)
2. What was the birth like? Did mom know what she wanted to do
   about this baby, as the birth was progressing?
3. What is his genetic makeup (responsible, in most cases, for
   46–51% of traits)? How have any genetic tendencies (for withdrawal, for aggression, for helplessness, for demandingness, etc.)
   interacted with his lived experience (of being unwanted, of
   being held or of being rarely touched, of having his dependency
   needs met or of being ignored, etc.)?
4. What were those 2-1/2 years with his birth family like? Did he
   have stable care, absent any losses or separations, from a very
   small group of primary caregivers who were irrationally in love
   with him? How stimulating was his world? How chaotic was his
   world? What were the family's beliefs about rocking, breastfeed-
   ing, responding to nighttime crying or terrors, holding and
   caressing—and what were their behaviors in these areas?
5. Why, ultimately, did he end up available for adoption?

Many of the questions above would also apply to the placements he
experienced before coming to your home. What caused each of those disruptions? Was loss starting to become familiar to Jonathon? More specifi-
cally, had he given up on attachment?

Only by understanding the answers to these questions—and many
more like them—is there any hope of really predicting what it will be like
for you and Paul to take him into your home, and hearts.

His behavior on the day he came to you (when he asked about Paul,
but not about the adoptive mother) may indicate that he finds safety in
your family, and did not in the former one. On the other hand, it may
indicate that he makes transitions suddenly, does not look back, that he is

promiscuous in his attachments (which are, by definition, then, superficial and self-serving). He may allow himself to fall into the bosom of the family, and change his mind about the narrative he had probably already written for his life. On the other hand, he may seem to be heading in that direction, only to respond shockingly to something as minor as seeing a lady at K-Mart that reminds him of his birthmother, or your family going on a trip (which makes him think of loss), or someone inadvertently hurting him (which could send him into a rage, the likes of which you have never seen).

I am glad to learn that your children are all older than Jonathon, as kids with his background often have profound tendencies to hurt children and animals smaller or younger than they are. So he may not be a physical danger to the rest of your family, at least for now. One of your other children may, however, tell you that he "sucks all the air out of the room"—meaning that the unpredictability of his behavior, or the chronicity of his behavior, or his constantly needing you to be "watching" him, or his tendency to create a swirl of chaos around him, may start wearing people out (your other kids, you, Paul).

On the other hand, it is just this sort of child that pulls our heartstrings the most, sometimes. There SEEMS to be so little wrong with him. Perhaps he will respond to love, and stability, and being valued. You can see how horribly he has been jerked around. Maybe you can even see that his behavior is not all that crazy, that it rather fits the story of his life. (For example: that he fights back against intimacy, because he is afraid he will lose it. Or that he will cuddle up to just about anyone, as if it really doesn't matter to whom he becomes attached. Or that he will fly into rages when he is injured or afraid, or even embarrassed, because he has had no defense against just those things in the past.)

Does he need you? Oh, goodness, that's the awful question. Of course he does. Big time. And certainly, as his placement history indicates, homes that could sustain themselves in the face of him and survive, homes that have what he needs, are few and far between. It will take a rare stamina to keep up with his needs and to keep your heads above water. But there is little that can save him EXCEPT what you have to offer. This doesn't mean you have to offer it, of course; you have to also be thoughtful about the many others who need you. (I suspect this is one of the things that gives Paul pause.) But he does need what you have.

I would be glad to share my film* (on the subject of children like Jonathon) with you, and I would also be glad to suggest other resources—readings, therapies, newsletters, etc.—but I don't want to overburden you

9

right away. And yes, because I, like you, love and trust Lindsay, I would make myself available for occasional consults like this one. My thoughts will be with you.

Michael Trout

*"Multiple Transitions: A Young Child's Point of View on Foster Care and Adoption", 16 minutes, VHS, produced by Michael Trout, available from The Infant-Parent Institute, 328 North Neil Street, Champaign, Illinois 61820 USA; tel: 217-352-4060; email: mtrout@infant-parent.com.

January 28, 2001

Dear Michael,

Thank you so much for your very thoughtful response to my plea for help! We really appreciate the fact that you have shared your time and expertise with us. You cannot imagine how timely your information was. Our "testing phase" has clearly begun.

You gave us a lot to digest. I know so little of Jonathon's past. Prenatal life: I know that Jonathon's birth mom was single, and 21. She had two elective abortions before he came along. There is nothing in the reports to suggest that she considered aborting him, but with her history I have to think that she might have struggled with that decision. There was no evidence or admission of drug or alcohol use during pregnancy.

Birth mom did keep Jonathon (more or less) for 2-1/2 years, rather than give him up at birth. To me, that suggests that she wanted him, but my mind and hers may not follow the same logic. And records indicate that Jonathon spent time with many different family members during those first 2-1/2 years.

Jonathon's birth mom went in for counseling, with the intention of giving him up for adoption, at around the time of his second birthday. She received help for 6 months, trying to learn to effectively parent him. After the 6 months, she stated that she was afraid that she would hurt him, and decided the time had come to relinquish parental rights.

Members of Jonathon's first foster family state that they really loved their time with him. He slept with a teenage foster brother, and did a lot of "male-bonding" there. Wrestling and roughhousing. That family included three sons (all older teens) one daughter (about 12, then) and a mom and a dad. There are photos of Jonathon sleeping on foster brother's chest. I think that his time there provided him a great deal of love.

His next family—the to-be adoptive family—did not seem like warm and cuddly types. They are a quiet, non-athletic, serene family. They wanted him to play violin and piano. When he frustrated them, they enrolled him in a strict, Catholic child-care center. He was there from 9 to 5, five days a week. Jonathon is a wild-child. Not a violin player type. To say the least, he was more the football player type.

Jonathon's behavior the past 24 hours has been pretty horrible: hiding from Paul, biting Rebecca, kicking and hitting. He has only acted this way towards the adult, authority figures. He has not hurt other children, or the dogs. In fact, he is very sensitive to Sugar, our very sick older dog. He refers to her as our broken dog, and he is very gentle with her.

Right now, all I want to do is hold Jonathon, rock him, and cry. I mourn for all he has suffered, and how that suffering causes all of us to suffer now. What has happened to him is so unfair. Life is not fair, but I hate that it can be SO unfair to a child. We will view the video that you sent, and devour any information that we can get our hands on, and pray.

Lindsay is indeed quite a special person in every respect. Her love for children, and especially for the special children of this world, is so clear in all that she does. We adore her.

I cannot tell you how much we appreciate your help. We know that Jonathon is special, and want to do everything we can to help him succeed.

From the bottom of our hearts, thank you,
Lori

January 29, 2001

Dear Lori,

Just a couple of thoughts, after reading your last communication:

A. What you had to say about his experience with being moved/jostled with/cuddled by the teen foster brother—then seriously frustrated in all of those areas in the subsequent adoptive home—is very important. I'm glad you know this, and that it means something to you.

For more documentation, and stories, about the extraordinary role played by these needs many boys have, you might want to take a look at *Real Boys*, a book by William Pollack. There are times when my youngest son (an 8-year-old adoptee with a horrid beginning) begs me to wrestle him—which usually does not actually mean "wrestling" in the customary sense but, rather, refers to his wish that I cuddle him hard, "squish" him (sort of like lying on him, often using a blanket), or pick him up. Sometimes he hates this; at other times, it is exactly what he wants, and seems to need. Kids like this often hate and mistrust their brains, and stay way out of touch with their hearts; but they can sometimes relax into pure motor activity, and even like to be overpowered (surprisingly).

B. Your observations about his not being a danger to small animals is important. While this is not an absolute, it is generally the case that children with attachment problems who are NOT violent with animals tend to NOT have full-blown, classic RAD (Reactive Attachment Disorder). This is extremely good news, potentially suggesting that he may be capable of human connections, that he may be able to rise above manipulative and superficial relationships.

C. There is a sense in which, of course, it is good that he is acting out. "Acting in" can be worse (tho' easier for parents to handle), as it usually leads either to serious clinical depression, or rage, or both. He is fighting for his life; he is fighting for psychological survival. It ain't pretty, and it is very difficult to hold on. And (I'll bet you have already guessed this) it may well get lots worse before it gets better. For the healthiest of these children (in other words: the ones who actually do have a soul, who are capable of love and connection), the terror approaches intolerability as they know more of the reliability of your love. It's an awful irony, I know: the better parents you are, the more you comfort him and allow him the opportunity to trust you, the worse his fear—and, therefore, his behavior—will get. If he has the inner workings of a full human being, there will be an end to this. It just won't happen fast, and it probably won't happen all at once but, rather, in frustrating fits and starts. (Just as you think things are getting better, he will devastate you with another meltdown.)

I hope this is not too much information/feedback, too fast. Your email was just so rich, I had to comment a little.

Michael Trout

January 30, 2001

Michael,

Thank you again for another timely response. You cannot imagine how much it meant to me last night to open my e-mails and have your information waiting.

Jonathon had a great day yesterday. We had a fairly quiet, unstructured day of play. No problems until...

Paul took Jonathon to a wrestling practice last night, which is an activity he loves. Jonathon and a 6-year-old girl usually wrestle together, and do quite well playing—until last night. They were rolling a roll of tape back and forth to each other, and then the little girl decided to keep it. Paul said that, in a matter of seconds, Jonathon had his sweater off and was hitting her with it as she cowered in a corner. She was crying, he was screaming. Paul immediately brought Jonathon home, and then returned to the practice.

Jonathon was crying loudly, and was very angry that Dad made him "... drop these wet tears on my face." His first words were about himself. "I wanted to stay there and play." "Dad is mean to me. You are mean, too. I want to go to another family." "I want to go back and play." He then moved into a remorse mode. "I don't want to be mean to my friends. I don't want to hurt them. She didn't let me say sorry. I want to say sorry." By this time, I was holding him tightly. He was lying on the couch, and I was next to him, wrapped around him. After his period of remorse, his sobbing became intense. His next words were: "I miss Ann. I want Ann." Ann is one of the nuns who worked with him at his daycare, and she is the one who wrote notes home daily. The notes were never objective, but full of obvious dislike for Jonathon, with phrases like, "He delights in tormenting... " and "He had another rotten day... " in every note. I cannot imagine, based on these notes, that there was much warmth in their relationship. In any case, Jonathon was crying about losing her. His next words were heartbreaking. "Why didn't she want me, Mom? Why didn't she want me?"

During last night's episode, I did not say much. I continued to hold him and rock him. When he would stop crying for a moment, I would say, "I love you, Jonathon." That was all I had to offer. I did not have answers for him, and did not feel he wanted any, anyway. He just needed to express his feelings and unload.

13

When Paul returned, he reported that the little girl would love to give Jonathon another chance, and still wanted to play with him again on Wednesday. Jonathon seemed happy to hear this. I suggested that he draw her a picture, and that he could try to be really nice next time. I said that he could come and tell us if he has problems, in the future.

After our bedtime ritual (which we did not follow closely one time, and we paid the price), I came in to read my e-mails, and there you were! It was such an encouragement, at a time when I was really drained. I think that Paul and I might need to get used to feeling drained! Seems to be a common occurrence these days. We are being stretched, and we are learning from it.

When Paul went back to the wrestling room last night, one of the other fathers reminded him of Helen Keller, her fits and frustration, and how she responded in time. It was good to hear another father who was willing to encourage Paul. He needed it!

Thanks again for everything!

Lori

February 1, 2001

Michael,

I just had a few thoughts that I wanted to pass along. Paul, Rebecca and I watched your video ["Multiple Transitions: A Young Child's Point of View on Foster Care and Adoption"—Ed.] two nights ago. Thank you for producing it, and for sharing it with us. As I reflected on it, I realized that much in there has been felt in this home already, and we have only had Jonathon for two weeks! I have heard Jonathon express some of those feelings, and felt the others with him. I do not know how to explain it, except to say that those thoughts are so strong that they manifest themselves very quickly. The depth of despair in these children is incredible.

We have already seen and raised so many children that I thought we had seen everything. Boy, was I wrong. At the same time, the fact that we have had a lot of experience parenting will help us through this. I really feel for parents who might be experiencing this with their first child.

James' original prognosis was very dire. (He is our adopted child from Korea, whom we share with Lindsay, as you are probably aware. She considers him hers, too. We love it that she loves him so.) James' diagnoses include autism, fetal alcohol syndrome, mild cerebral palsy, microcephaly, atrophied cerebellum, and Tourette's Syndrome. As a result of those problems, of course, we have others: seizure activity, mental retardation, speech delay, small motor difficulties. When we first met James (we lived in Korea at the time) we brought him into our home and took him to our American doctors. They advised against adoption, and told us that his chances of bonding, learning, speaking, walking, and the like were not good. James has proven them wrong. He is a walking, running, loving, busy boy. He brings happiness to more people than the rest of my family, combined, could ever do. He just touches people's hearts in incredible ways.

I know that I am mixing apples and oranges, and that I should be careful about doing that, but James' progress gives me more hope for Jonathon. The human spirit is strong, and God's power is even stronger.

If I can ever help to encourage other parents, I would be happy to do so. I know that our path, and struggle, with Jonathon is just beginning. I understand (fearfully) that things will get worse before they get better. And then maybe they will get worse again. I do not have any clue how we will do as we go through these times. I hope to learn as we go. However, I have seen incredible miracles in other children, and would be happy to share that encouraging word with others.

A quick question: Do you know of any books that tell the story of people with attachment disorders who went on to live productive lives? That would be nice reading right now. I thought of *A Child Called It, The Lost Boy,* and *A Man Called Dave.* I devoured those books last year, and have to think that the character in them must have had attachment problems. I think I will re-read them.

Thanks again for all of your help.

Very appreciatively,
Lori

February 4, 2001

Dear Lori,

I had the oddest thought after reading your latest communication. In just these few days, we have talked about a great many important things, while a process takes hold in your family that has included anticipation, fear, faith, wonderment, terror, hope, prognostication. It dawns on me— imagining another parent in your position reading what we have said to each other—that these exchanges (should they continue) might be a source of information and inspiration to others. This would most assuredly remain the case if these exchanges included stories of everything going sour, or of the placement collapsing; in other words, their use would NOT be dependent on their having a "happy ending". In any case, I'm going to retain copies of what we have said to each other, and may someday come back to you with an idea…

The author of the books you mentioned (Dave Pelzer), and I, spoke at the same conference, in Detroit, a year or so ago. While Dave's experience was certainly horrific, I suspect it differs in some respects from the experience you are going to have with Jonathon. His was, in some respects, from a "normal" family. They had resources, two parents, employment, and the cover of neighborhood and community. Dave got out by the skin of his teeth, but at an advanced age, and after developing profound inner resources to cope. Jonathon, and thousands of other little ones like him, certainly developed inner resources to cope with their pain, but these were largely primitive resources (dissociation, hardening, development of a "false self", etc.) that helped them to avoid further pain and to attract alternative care. It's a tough call to say whose situation is "worse"; that's a comparison it seems inhumane to make. In terms of the seriousness of the internal damage, however, it seems likely that the Daves of the world have a better chance.

With respect to your question about a book that suggests a happy outcome, I might suggest that you contact The Attachment Center at Evergreen in Colorado [now known as the Institute for Attachment and Child Development]. They have a newsletter worth subscribing to, and can put you in touch with suggested readings and other resources. Perhaps I will send you some materials tomorrow, when I get to the office, which might give you some additional ideas.

Your comparison of James and Jonathon reminds me of my own struggle, with the families that come to me, to understand (sometimes retrospectively) what happened to a particular child, so we can know whether he will turn out to be a James, or a Jonathon, or yet another type of child. The answers lie in all of those questions I posed to you in one of my first communications. It is simply astonishing, sometimes, to see what a huge difference is made by something seemingly minor in the history. I am presently working with a couple that adopted two boys from the same orphanage in the Philippines, at the same time, at the same age. They were not brothers, but most all the superficial data about their backgrounds was similar. Now, at age 14, they could not possibly resemble each other less. One is happy, competent, and self-confident. The other is morose, angry, and absolutely lacking in any strong sense of self. The parents were at a loss to understand this, until they began to consider seriously this difference: the depressed child came to America with no one, and began screaming the minute he was placed in his adoptive mother's arms. He could not be comforted. The other child was accompanied to America (on the very same plane) by a young girl who had looked after him in the Philippine orphanage. The adoptive parents liked her so much that they invited her to stay with them—for 2 1/2 years! She continued to be this child's surrogate "mother", and slowly transitioned out of the family when he was a happy and secure two-year-old.

My best to you and Paul,
Michael Trout

February 5, 2001

Michael,

I would be thrilled to have these exchanges continue, and for them to be used in a way to help others in the future!

Saturday evening I escaped to Barnes and Noble, one of my favorite spots in the whole world. I needed to escape to recharge myself. I found *Real Boys*, as you recommended, as well as *The Things I Want Most*, by Richard Miniter, and *Orphan*, by Roger Dean Kiser, Sr. Maybe I am drawn to them because the characters in them, like Dave, seem to come out okay. I want that to be our ending, too.

Jonathon is sick today: high fever, flu symptoms. He is so sweet and cuddly. I do not want him to be sick, by I am enjoying the time to hold him and know him as a quiet child. Is this the child that, properly treated, he could be, full-time? I really like this child!

It is impossible to not love Jonathon. He has been through so much, and is so needy, and he needs to be loved. Therefore, we love him. And he does have truly loveable moments. Sometimes, however, he makes it very hard to like him. Love is a decision; like is an emotion. Like is harder. Today, I like Jonathon. I want to always like him.

Lori

February 5, 2001

Dear Lori,

I was going to send you a couple of newsletters that will help you to know of some of the resources out there, and realized I did not have your mailing address.

Would Paul ever feel comfortable chatting a bit about how all of this is for him? I don't mean to be intrusive, but I also don't want to bypass, overlook or in any way discount him. If we continue this episodic consulting, it seems that I ought to "know" him a little, and he me.

Michael Trout

February 6, 2001

Michael,

Lori has kept me up-to-date on her correspondence with you, and I would be happy to chip in with my thoughts.

Let me start by stating that I believe Jonathon has many positive character traits. They are his engaging personality, often-friendly disposition, and loving attitude toward animals, among others. He also has some significant flaws: unrepentant attitude after disobedience, willfulness in pursuit of his desires, and a tendency towards tantrums and physical exhibition of displeasure, among others.

Jonathon started out with about 24 hours of good behavior, and then moved into a phase of direct confrontation. He generally chose to battle over parental direction to end an activity that he wanted to continue. Jonathon would ignore direction and, when pressed, seek to get away from the parent. In each instance I was able to immediately catch him and impose my will. He realized after about 19 days that that approach would not work.

Once the intermittent, overt defiance ended (at least for now), Jonathon switched to more subtle methods. For instance, he will pretend that he does not hear direction, or will put on an angry face and sulk. He also tries to win little battles, such as not eating his food or not picking up messes. I try to be consistent and clearly state the rules, but am forgiving once he shows he understands. Jonathon is already much more able to take direction, and reacts positively to "no".

I have worked hard to get him to cuddle. At first his only physical contact with me was in the form of "wrestling" (generally well-controlled). Now he is much more willing to sit on my lap to watch a show.

I am now trying to get him to let go of things, rather than ask for things over and over. For example, when we are getting close to dinner, he starts saying he is hungry, every 2 minutes or so. I want him to eat dinner, so ask him to wait. So far, little progress.

Hope this is helpful,
Paul

February 14, 2001

Dear Michael,

Just a quick note to let you know how things are going here. First, let me thank you for sending those newsletters. They are very helpful. We have been devouring any information we find... on the web, in those newsletters.

We have had an excellent week. Minor defiance (at least compared to what we were experiencing) and difficulty with transition are our major issues right now. On a scale of 1–10, with 10 being unbearable, we have been in the 2 scale. A week ago I would have placed us on the 6 or 7 scale. This current peaceful phase scares me. I do not want to take for granted that things will continue. I am sure that the minute my guard is down, all heck will break loose. Isn't that ironic? Isn't that exactly why kids like Jonathon can't bond? I am sure that, at least on a subconscious level, Jonathon does not want to let his guard down and bond. After all, that is when he will get hurt again. Bond, lose, and hurt. Not worth the risk. So the children cannot relax and bond, and the parents cannot relax and enjoy peace when it is offered. Kind of a vicious cycle, eh? Everyone is expecting terror

around the corner. But we will learn from each other, get to know each other better, and come to a point where we can move forward in a healthy way.

We will start therapy with an Attachment Disorder therapist on Monday. Siobhan, a good friend of Lindsay and the Thomas family, recommended this therapist. On the phone, he sounds wonderful. I am excited.

Do you hear the optimism in my e-mail voice? I will save this e-mail, and re-read it when I need it.

Lori

February 15, 2001

Dear Lori,

I was thinking about how profound is your notice of the cycle, about "terror around the corner". I suspect that thousands of foster placements have disrupted on the head of that very pin, as the two terrified partners collided. So, perhaps there must be a rule: "One of us can be afraid at a time"!

Transitions never cease to be a problem in our house, too, with 8-year-old Jeremy (adopted at 8 months of age, from a horrid Guatemalan foster home). If he happens to be the last one out of the car, in the garage, he is prone to collapse into full-blown terror, shrieking that we have left him. Remembering to give advance-notice, lots of talk, sitting with him as he shrieks, trying to remind him about what he is really feeling, and consoling him that we will never leave—all of these, after a few years, have finally helped him to have fewer and fewer meltdowns.

Speaking of helping Jeremy to find words for what he is really feeling: This is, of course, a major deficiency in children with RAD, almost by definition. While Jonathon is too young for this, at the moment, I should mention that our Jeremy seems to have made quantum leaps since we began using little laminated cards with simple drawings of faces, and a one-word (per card) descriptor about a feeling. We pull them out when he is melting down, and ask him to just point to a card, or to sort through them until he finds one that seems right as a description of his feeling at the moment. We are surprised that he does not resist too strongly (tho' he gives the obligatory sigh and slams the cards around before getting down to business), indicating to me that he knows they help. It almost seems a relief to him to find that there is a word to describe what is inside him at the moment, and that other people know the word, too—which implies, I suppose, that it is acceptable to have such a feeling, and he will not die or kill anyone else by having it.

I will be thinking of Jonathon, and you all, as you begin work with a therapist on Monday.

Michael Trout

February 23, 2001

Michael,

Attachment Therapy really is WORK, isn't it? We all left our first session drained. If our therapist had not been recommended to us by people I trust, I would have been tempted to leave about half way through our session. The intensity of Jonathon's struggle was incredible, and I had my doubts. I remember thinking, during the session, that Jonathon would never want to come back or talk to this man again, due to Jonathon's resistance to work with us during the therapy. After our session was over, however, Jonathon was happy to chat with our therapist and clearly had no ill feelings towards him, personally. He seemed relieved to have let some emotions out, and to have even had the "mad" and "sad" identified. He was very willing to stay and talk for a few more minutes. He did, however, announce to the therapist that we would not be coming back. It was a matter-of-fact statement. Jon said, "I will see you all next week". Jonathon very nicely told him that no, we would not be there. I think I can expect some resistance from Jonathon on Monday, but we will be there. After our first session, we stopped for lunch on the way home. Jonathon was very clingy to me, and very quiet and subdued for most of the day.

We are excited about this work, and the potential it has for Jonathon, and for us as we explore adding Jonathon to our family on a permanent basis.

This has been an up-and-down week for Jonathon. We had a major episode of tantrums when a friend of mine came over for a visit. Jonathon was sitting with me, and we all visited. My friend tends to be loud, and Jonathon got clingy. Then he just had a huge meltdown, and started screaming. It was a difficult night for all of us. My friend is African-American, as is Jonathon. This is the second time he had a major melt-down around loud, African-American people. Another friend, who is the same race but soft-spoken, has never triggered a negative response from him. I really do think he was triggered by something about my friend. I know that his birth grandmother was loud and domineering.

Unfortunately, my friend did not handle Jonathon's melt-down well. She decided that I was being mistreated (Jonathon was kicking), and told Jonathon so. Then she threatened to lock him in his room. I was furious. She left, and I did my best to calm Jonathon down. I showed him the door to his room, and that there was no lock on it. I told him that I would NEVER let anyone lock him in any room. It took hours for him to calm down, and then

I remained furious at my friend for hours after that. Why do people think they have the right to interfere in the discipline of other people's children? I can see that having a child like Jonathon is going to keep me on my toes in many areas. Clearly, I need to be very wise about which friends have access to my children. So much damage can be done by such thoughtless acts and comments.

My friend claims that she was just "testing" him. She knows a child with attachment disorder, and that child would really have a fit if someone mentioned locking him into a room. So she says she was testing to see if Jonathon really has an attachment disorder. She thinks that maybe he doesn't, but is just seeking attention. Do I need to say it again? I was/am furious. I suppose she meant well, but I do not need that kind of help.

I mentioned in an earlier communication that Jonathon has been kind to our dogs. That has remained, for the most part, true. He clearly loves Gidget, our black lab. (Sugar, our German Shepherd, died on Monday.) I have seen him hit her with toys, but never really aggressively. He hugs and kisses her constantly. I was not worried about his hurting her. But today, he did something unexpected.

Jonathon, James, and Gidget were all downstairs, watching a video. Rebecca walked in and found Jonathon urinating on Gidget. I believe it is the first time he has done that. There are reports from his last home of masturbation in inappropriate places (dinner table) and some bed-wetting. He has not done either of those things here. I am not sure what to make of this episode. I feel inclined to not worry unless I see this behavior repeated. We did not make a huge deal about it today. He had to help clean up the mess, and we let him know that we will have to watch him more carefully when he wants to play with Gidget. Part of me wants to worry, look for signs of sexual abuse in his past, and so on. The other part wants to remember that he is a 4-1/2-year-old boy, and some behaviors are just part of growing up and experimenting. So we won't panic, and we will keep our eyes open. Sound like the right approach?

Jonathon has been with us five weeks now. I can honestly say that I am exhausted, hopeful, happy, sad, excited, nervous, and confused. I try to remember that each day is a victory. We are learning, loving, and surviving. Each twenty-four hour period puts us one day closer to our time of attachment. The road ahead is long, but each step we take makes the road behind us a bit longer, too. The further along the road we get, the more committed we are to our journey. If only our destination were marked a bit more clearly. I hope we will recognize it when we get there.

Thank you for sharing about your stepson, Jeremy. It helps just to know that there are others going through the same thing.

You are on our "to be thankful for" list!
Lori

February 27, 2001

Dear Lori,

Some amazing things "friends" think they have permission to do, eh? So she was "experimenting" with your child—messing with someone's mind and heart—without asking your permission, or his?

I do, of course, understand what you mean about the attachment therapy being WORK. There are times when you may have to bite more than your lips to hold yourself on the parents' side of the mirror, or to avoid grabbing Jonathon up in your arms and running out. It is very hard to keep imagining how badly Jonathon may be plagued by/threatened by/frightened to death of his own insides—his impulses, his rage—and, therefore, how much he needs someone(s) to protect him from those very impulses and that very rage.

I would not suggest you frame the urination-on-the-dog episode as developmentally appropriate, as another "boys will be boys" or "four-year-olds will be four-year-olds" event. At the core of this behavior is an absence of awareness of another as AN OTHER. Kids with RAD typically do not quite "get" the boundaries between themselves and others, even in physical terms. It is legendary that these kids can walk across the room stepping on baby's hand, the dog's face and Dad's foot, and never know they have made human contact at all. They are capable of injuring without awareness. This looks different from the child who seems to injure with intent to harm, with apparent rage and aggressiveness. But the origins are the same. If you add to the mix the possibility of an absence of empathy for the OTHER ("What does it feel like to be peed on?"), the mix is insidious.

Still, other four-year-olds sometimes do similar things. They can be thoughtless, unaware, clumsy, and insensitive. The line is not heavy and black (between typical and atypical).

What reaction did you notice to Sugar's death? A peculiar fact about some children with RAD is that they do not appear to grieve at all—except via their behavior. Rare is the parent who can make the connection between loss and a behavior change, since we are usually looking for grief behavior that resembles our own, rather than that which fits the defensive structure of the child.

You are courageous people. Jonathon is blessed by your faith.
Michael Trout

March 1, 2001

Michael,

What a week we have had! I think I say that a lot these days!

Jonathon's response to Sugar's death has been interesting. He speaks for Gidget a lot. He gets next to her, and says in his puppy-dog voice, "I miss Sugar. I want Sugar to come back." He also wants to know if we are going to visit her in heaven. He has been very devoted to Gidget, giving her lots of hugs and attention. He has not increased his "acting-out" behaviors, which I would have expected.

If emotions were allowed to rule us, I would be completely insane by now. Jonathon's feelings are so very "all over the place". In the past, Jonathon always has announced that he is ready to move to another house whenever he is being disciplined for his behavior. Monday is the first time that he has mentioned moving to another house during a peaceful, happy time. We were playing quietly on the floor, and all was well. Then Jonathon said, "It is too boring here.

"Yesterday we were playing on the floor, and Jonathon said, 'It is too boring here. I think I will go to my next house now."

25

I think I will go to my next house now." I am sure that his response was due to a feeling of closeness, and his fear of that closeness. That was on Monday.

Tuesday we went to our home-school co-op group. I was teaching the 4th, 5th and 6th graders, and I took Jonathon to his age group first. The teacher in his class this week was black. Jonathon said that he did not want to stay, and was rather insistent that I come out in the hall to talk to him. Once in the hallway, he pulled me down and whispered into my ear, "Mom, if you can find a white woman to stay with me, I will stay. But I will not stay with a black woman. I do not like black women." (Jonathon is black.) I did find a white woman, a good friend of ours, to stay in there for a few minutes to try to transition him. Of course, once it was time for her to leave, he left with her. They came to my room, and my friend asked if Jonathon could go home with her during our class time. I gave permission, and Jonathon went with her happily. As they were walking, holding hands, Jonathon asked her if he could call her "Mom". She said that he already has a Mom who loves him, and that it might hurt my feelings if he called her "mom". He was okay with that. That was Tuesday.

Wednesday, during another quiet playtime, Jonathon came and sat on my lap. He looked up at me with his big eyes and asked "Mom, can I stay here forever?" I told him that I love him, and that that would make me happy. I would have been thrilled if I thought it meant anything. Some day, I believe he will say that and mean it. Right now, it is just another idea on another day. One day he is leaving, the next day he wants to call a friend of mine "mom", and then he wants to stay here forever. Such confusion reigns in his precious mind. I wonder what "forever" means to him.

We will probably begin twice-a-week therapy this week. Jon feels that Jonathon's resistance level is quite high. We have only had two sessions, so it will be interesting to see what effect this will have on him. I remain very excited and hopeful about the therapy.

Here's hoping for a survivable week!
Lori

March 5, 2001

Lordy, such a roller-coaster ride! Perhaps you are communicating to me, however, that you are working on not going so high OR so low. It can wear a person out...

When your core work is slowly challenging the very story line of Jonathon's life—that which he has "written on his soul" in order to better understand what was happening to him and to let him imagine he had SOME control, when very small—then everything takes on a very different tone than if you were merely loving and teaching a regular child, doesn't it? You seem to be rearranging your expectations, so as to be in synchrony with the work of his heart. Therefore, nothing you experience today should be presumed to be anything more than that which is happening today. Then, if it happens two days in a row, the presumptions must be limited to the notice that it has happened two days in a row. This way of thinking flies in the face of how much we want to see patterns, to be affirmed that change is happening.

But it is a genuinely perplexing question: How much can a parent move with a child, when, in alternating minutes, the child:

A. says "I love you"; then

B. hits at you; then

C. climbs on your lap and cuddles; then

D. calls you vile names; then

E. tells you some horrific tale about life in the birth home, or in a previous foster home, that pulls on every empathic string in your body, and makes you want to "save" him from all harm; then

F. asks some lady he has just met if he can call her "mom", and seems quite willing to follow her home; then

G. tells you no one ever made him cookies before; then

H. stuffs handfuls of said cookies down the throat of a baby or a kitten in the family while smiling and saying—over the gags of the baby or the kitten—that he is "sharing", or that your cookies are the stupidest cookies he has ever seen and he will never eat them.

"The stress of Jonathon is starting to take its toll. I am pretty sure a move to some distant land would be a great idea. I am beginning to wonder if this placement is going to work."

I suspect many placements have disrupted not over a crisis, per se, but just when all of this unpredictability and lack of steady progress toward some kind of goal got, finally, to be too much, on one particular day. I admire your multiple levels of work, including your restructuring expectations, finding some way to get through today, finding some way to find hints of something one might reasonably call "progress", without investing too much in the permanence of it. I would love you to tell me someday, if you know, what the key elements of your survival have been.

I'm intrigued by Jonathon's speaking for Gidget. This might just turn out to be an important inroad to his own heart: He may describe his own feelings by projecting them onto Gidget, then speaking empathically "for" her. Amazing. (One of the most compelling revelations of my stepson Jeremy's feelings came about one night while I was exercising—perhaps, for him, a safer time to talk to me, while I was not wholly concentrating on him—and he did all his talking through this goofy "wig hat" he has. He took it off, chatted with it, held it up to his ear, then told me what the hat said to him. Knocked me out.)

My best... Michael

March 8, 2001

Michael,

Thank you again for another timely correspondence. I laughed so hard while reading the "talking hat" episode. It really hit me since I am living that "projected speech" life right now.

Last week, the tension in our home was reaching an unbearable limit. We have always had an easy-going, wonderful relationship with our children. None of us is perfect, but we certainly counted ourselves among the happy and well-adjusted families of the world. Suddenly, the stress of Jonathon started to take its toll. I was pretty sure a move to some distant land (just me, by myself) was a great idea. We were all so very frustrated, and trying not to place that frustration on Jonathon. I began to wonder if this placement was, indeed, going to work. It was the first time (but it will probably not be the last) that I had doubts. On Sunday, the sermon was about dealing with stress.

It was perfect for us. Then, the pastor made a great point. He asked us to really consider our priorities. Were we stressed by things that were not important, eternally? Working overtime just to have a bigger house? Or were we doing something that we really believed in, something that would count for eternity? I evaluated my stress, and realized that I am willing to give up a great deal of comfort in order to reach Jonathon. I am not willing to risk my family, but I am willing to be out of my comfort zone. So the key is to figure out how to minimize the toll on the family, while still working effectively with Jonathon.

I came to some conclusions. It has taken me 6-1/2 weeks, but I finally get it! The "good parenting" that I have done with my other children will not work for Jonathon. He is different, and I have to parent differently! Intellectually, I understood that before. I tried to change my style enough to get through to Jonathon. But now I really understand. I need to radically change the way I do things!!

Every day is a 24-hour therapy opportunity, and I must take advantage of that. To reach this child will be much more than work. It will be constant work, and a change of attitude in our discipline. I am reading Building the Bonds of Attachment (Daniel Hughes). I just started, but think it will be a very helpful resource of ideas in parenting.

An analogy occurred to me as I was dressing for my doctor appointment this morning. I have recurring bronchitis and pneumonia. I developed this problem while living in Korea. My lungs could not adjust to the pollution and irritants in the air there, and I developed asthma. The asthma led to other problems and, suddenly, I was very sick with pneumonia. I developed a severe case, which did not respond to the normal antibiotics. It took 3 months to get the pneumonia cleared up, and my body healthy again. Unfortunately, scarring on my lungs remains. Although it can be managed, my lungs will never be the same again. I have a tendency to develop bronchitis and pneumonia very easily now, and have to always be on guard. So the analogy: Jonathon is like my lungs. The damage has been done to his soul, and he will always be at risk. Once we make a break-through, we will learn to manage (and help him learn to manage) his behavior and his feelings. He will, hopefully, be able to learn to live a happy life. He will, however, be more vulnerable than the "normal" child out there, and will need to be on guard. Is this a valid analogy? Do my lungs and Jonathon have something in common, and will the risk remain forever? From what I have read, I think I know the answer.

I was thinking again about the differences between James and Jonathon. James came to us very broken, but empty. He did not make eye contact, did not make noise, and had completely given up on human interaction. He spent most of his time rocking back and forth, flipping through a magazine. Once we reached him, and bonding began, it was like filling up an empty vessel. He was responsive and ready to be loved. He did not resist the love, he just had not realized it was out there. It was hard work, but a joy to watch the progress.

Jonathon's case is so different. He resists attempts to reach him with every ounce of energy he has. There is so much damage to undo. He isn't empty, but full of self-hatred and the "knowledge" that he is not loveable. He was asked today, in therapy, why he ran away from me yesterday in a crowd. He said he wanted me to chase him. Jon then asked him what he was thinking. He says he was thinking that I would get mad and give him away now. He was asked if he deserved to be loved. "No", was his answer. Could he trust his birth mom? "Yes", he said, and she did the right thing to give him away. After he ran from me, I realized that we have repeated our "normal" discipline cycle too many times. It occurred to me that I needed to stop right there and get control of the situation and of both of us. So I grabbed him, sat down right there with him, and held him. There was no quiet place to go, so I just held him there. I told him how sorry I was that he had not learned not to run from me yet, and that I would need to hold him to keep him and the other people safe. He hated being restrained. He really wanted me to chase him, scold him, and let him go so that he could repeat the behavior and control our day. I am catching on, slowly.

So, slowly we learn, but we are trainable! (I hope so, anyway.) We have talked with our other kids about our approach to Jonathon, and told them that we want everyone to be more relaxed. We discussed our new approach (no anger, more holding and gentle correcting, and working through the consequences with Jonathon: strict, but calm) and asked for their cooperation. I think we are off to a good re-start.

I'll let you know how things go.
Lori

March 16, 2001

Michael,

I want to send a quick update for two reasons: to get your input, if possible, on some new behaviors; and to put it into print, in order to get it off my mind. Make sense?

Jonathon's resistance has dramatically increased in the past week. I have been doing a lot of "therapeutic holding", and have allowed Jonathon less freedom. I feel like we are on the right track. Since beginning that, we have seen his behavior worsen. I think you warned me about that very thing. I think he is fighting for control, and he is scared to lose it. He does not know, yet, that it is okay for Mom to have control, and that things will work better that way.

Last night I found Jonathon and James playing "boyfriend and girlfriend" in bed together. They had both been tucked in for the night, and I was doing one of my frequent checks, while waiting for them to fall asleep. They had both partially undressed, and Jonathon said he was "...pretending to eat James' bottom". There were red marks on James' buttocks, but no teeth marks. This morning, the marks are gone. Jonathon also said that he was kissing James' cheek, but not his mouth, because "...mouths have germs". When I found the boys, I stayed calm. I dressed them both again, and tucked James back into his bed. I then held Jonathon for awhile, rocked him, and firmly explained that they may not play boyfriend and girlfriend anymore. Jonathon shared with me some times he had played that with a friend of his, while he was living in his last home. I gently prodded, and did not get any indication that any adult had done anything with Jonathon, sexually.

Oops, just ran out of time. Got a call from Lindsay, saying that we forgot to give James his medicine this morning! He is currently sitting atop his desk. Off to school we go.

Lori

March 20, 2001

Dear Lori,

No, my courageous friends, you are not catching on slowly. You are catching on more rapidly than you can imagine, and more deeply than many struggling parents can/do in a lifetime. Your use of metaphor (especially to explain things to yourselves, and to see things more clearly) is going to prove a great aide, I am sure. It helps the principles to emerge more clearly (Example: "Jonathon wants to run away, but he also wants to be chased and caught; my job is to come down on the latter side of him."), see damage in a clearer light and in a proper perspective ("My lungs will never be the same, but they are far from useless, and I can learn/adapt.")

It is amazing how a child so injured can seek (with astounding success, often) to injure others. More particularly, I hear your report that Jonathon may have begun to go after the "heart", the safety, maybe even the integrity of the family. These things about your family he hates, of course—that there IS a heart to it, that there IS integrity and safety in it—because he knows he did not have these things in his original family (or in any subsequent one?). These are also things he needs, desperately—much the same as how badly he needs to be held and touched, yet how fiercely he keeps you from doing it. So he will find every sore in the family—including those you didn't even know you had—and pick at them quietly (alright, sometimes not so quietly) until they bleed. Then he will rejoice, and pick at the scab. He must make every member of the family feel as he did/does. It is essential to his survival (he imagines). You will, as a result, begin noticing divisions among yourselves. You may notice some withdrawals, irritability, anger.

I say all of this not to dissuade, and certainly not to be dramatic but, instead, to normalize the experience it sounds as if you are already having. He needs to fail in this quest, of course. He needs to be unsuccessful in driving you and your husband apart even in the slightest. He needs to see that he cannot get you yelling at your other kids, or picking sides, or changing standards too much. He needs, ironically, to feel impotent in his moves to disable the family.

I remember watching my stepson, Jeremy—when he was about six, and I had just met his mother—ram his bicycle into her because she declined to carry it for him. Her ankle was bleeding, but he didn't seem to notice or care, and he went on raging and threatening her. She was trying so hard to be "nice" and understanding of this poor child, who had had such a rotten beginning. What she overlooked was how terrified his behavior made him. His impulses raged inside, and they were his enemy. He made out that SHE was, of course—or anyone else who crossed him. But it was his own insides (including his hurt, his fury, his wish to die, his wish to kill, his inability to articulate any of it) that really stood in the way of his entering the world, of learning to love or to accept love. Jeremy was instructed on that day that he would no longer be permitted to hurt anyone. We said that we knew he did not want to hurt (not entirely true, of course), and that he needed our help to stop. So he would get our help. No one would be permitted to hurt him, and he would be permitted to hurt no one. To our astonishment, he has stopped. Oh, not right away. (Did you think this a fairy tale?!) But he no longer hits at school, and the thrashing/kicking/screaming/fist-throwing against his mother went away within about six months.

The very same principle probably applies relative to the wish to run away, to avoid intimacy, etc.: It is our job to help him "win" the struggle with his own insides that would deny him what he really wants (safety, intimacy, family). We expect it to be a fight, but we are bigger and stronger than his impulses.

Michael

March 21, 2001

Michael,

On 8 March I wrote to you of our frustrations, and our realization that we needed to start over with a new approach. We had just started using lots of therapeutic holding, and the "attitude" that accompanies it, with Jonathon. This immediately worked wonders for me. My tension, and that of the family, was instantly reduced. There was no noticeable change in Jonathon, initially, but my first priority was to get the family back in unity, working as a team. Once everyone understood our new game plan, it was much easier to get through each day. For the first week, we experienced huge resistance from Jonathon. I am now pretty good at holding him, but I have some good bruises to prove that it took practice before I learned to quickly gain control of Jonathon's arms and legs. Lots of screaming (by Jonathon, not me) and crying (by both), and some pretty good struggles ensued. In the end, we always ended with good contact (eyes, words, emotions) and I felt good about the process.

After the first week, Jonathon's resistance lessened. His behavior did not improve, but his desire to control the holding time diminished just a bit. About this point, Paul expressed his concern to me that this new pattern of correcting and teaching Jonathon was not working. He was not too sure if we were on the right track, but he encouraged me to continue for a bit longer. We are both trying to learn as we go.

Suddenly, last week, Jonathon's general demeanor changed the tiniest bit. The way he held on to me was a bit more intense. His eye contact increased a little. These were very subtle changes, but they gave us some hope that something wonderful was happening in our little boy. I know it has only been a little more than two months since Jonathon came to us, and I know that this might sound kind of crazy, but I really believe that Jonathon is starting to allow himself to attach to us. Let me give you an example of what I am seeing.

Jonathon has not been much fun to take out in crowds. His behavior has been to run, hide, and see if we could find him. He would hide around a corner, step out of a door, or anything that seemed fun to him at that moment. In his last home, it is reported that he jumped into the door of a bus and almost got away! He has not shown any fear of separation. It has been a nerve-racking experience to go out with him, and we have recently limited our outings to allow him a chance to succeed at home. Anyway, on this past Saturday, we had a trip to the Baltimore Aquarium planned. It has been planned for quite some time, but I was debating canceling it. I just did not think that Jonathon was ready. I did not want to disappoint the rest of the family, so I decided to go ahead on the outing, sure that I would hate myself later for that decision. I thought I was setting us all up for disaster. But I was wrong. Jonathon stayed very close to us the whole day, always making sure that he had either my hand or Paul's. He clung to us like a little boy who didn't want to lose his family. It was incredible!

So we are cautiously optimistic, and pretty darn happy. We want this to work so very, very much. I am starting to think that "Jonathon Thomas" has a nice ring to it.

Ralph Waldo Emerson wrote, "This time, like all times, is a very good one, if we but know what to do with it." I do not want to waste today, as I wait for the miraculous healing that will take place tomorrow. There is joy in today, too. So... we will work hard for the future, but we will also savor each day and the small steps that we witness.

We were touched by your last correspondence, and your use of the words "courageous friends". Courageous we are not, but we are honored to be called your friends! Thanks so much for being there.

Lori

March 22, 2001

Dear Lori,

Your words reminded me of several amazing things I have learned from the families whom I have witnessed trying to love and to parent children like Jonathon over these years:

A. Time passes quickly, even tho' it often seems to grind along. Such a paradox.

B. It can feel wonderful to have a plan. Even if it later turns out that it was not a perfect plan—or even that it was wrong—it feels SO much better to know SOMETHING specific and definitive to DO when there is a meltdown, or a runaway, or other seemingly random, crazy behaviors.

C. Patterns start to become more apparent. But, perhaps most importantly, it gives us some sense that the chaos is less, that we are HEADING somewhere, and our present behaviors are part of a larger plan.

D. Our detection systems (for noticing the most minute changes) become finely-honed. Perhaps it is what happened to all of us when we first became parents and discovered that our sleep would never be the same again, since we could now detect a change in the breathing of a child two rooms away, in the middle of the night. I hear you clearly when you describe the tiniest shift in Jonathon in recent days.

I thought I would fall over laughing at your report that "... Jonathon wasn't usually much fun to take into crowds". A hundred pictures came into my mind: of children running away (and our often-pathetic struggle to chase); of children kicking their mothers in the parking lot; of a child going into total, unrestrained meltdown in the middle of a lobby, with at least 500 gaping, dumbstruck adults staring, judging, condemning. Yes, you probably are nuts (is there any other way to parent-for-growth?), but ZOWIE, it must have been something to experience his behaving differently, just for that day.

My best.
Michael

March 24, 2001

Michael,

Just a quick note from our part of the country to yours. First, let me explain what I mean by, "Jonathon was not usually much fun to take into crowds":

1. I would rather suffer at the dentist than take Jonathon into a crowded place.
2. I would be more comfortable going through childbirth than taking Jonathon into a room full of people.
3. I now understand why people use those child "leashes".
4. Being the mother of Jonathon, I am sorely tempted to become agoraphobic.

Anyway, you get the idea. But our aquarium experience WAS a real treat. I am looking forward to more just like it. I do not know when or how, but I trust that more great days are ahead—interspersed, of course, with some rotten ones.

Today, Jonathon and I went on a field trip with Rebecca's high school. He was quite the entertainment for the "big kids", and mostly that was a good thing. We did not have any trouble keeping him with us, which was wonderful. He had a minor meltdown at lunchtime but, other than that, he handled the outing very well.

Tomorrow we are celebrating Jonathon's 5th birthday! Lindsay will be here for our party. She has not seen Jonathon for a couple of weeks, so I am looking forward to her observations of him and any changes she sees. We have not invited a big crowd, but one of Jonathon's former foster families will be there. We had a wonderful visit with them two weeks ago, and he invited them to his party very willingly. I am hoping it is not too much for him. I think that seeing someone from his past, enjoying them, and then returning home with us again, was a very good thing.

Hope you have a great weekend! I will let you know how my almost five-year-old handles ours.

Lori

March 26, 2001

Michael,

Here is our situation: We all love Jonathon, and WE are very capable of bonding. We know that he has the potential to attach, as we see it taking place on a small scale already. We feel strong enough as a family to endure the tough times, and flexible enough as a family to see the humor in our current situation (meaning, of course, that every time our family seems to get to a very peaceful phase, something or someone comes along to stir us all up just a bit). We cannot imagine our family without Jonathon, and we cannot imagine Jonathon without our family. Therefore, we really have no choice!

Back to the weekend: Friday was the day that Grandma came, so it was a change in the routine and therefore a bit hectic for Jonathon and James. By Saturday, James was loving Grandma very much, and Jonathon was still a very hyper little boy. I spent some time holding him and trying to calm him before his party. I failed in the calming department. By the time people arrived, Jonathon was quite anxious to open gifts, play, talk non-stop, and be a touch disobedient. There were several times when I would have, under normal circumstances, taken Jonathon aside for holding time. I should have done exactly that, but felt impotent as his mother, with all the people from his past here. His wonderful former foster family was here, and I don't know if they are familiar with the type of therapy and parenting that we are using for Jonathon. In addition to that, our social worker was here. She has not been to a therapy session with us yet, and I do not know how she would respond to our holding times. I just was not comfortable, and it was a horrible feeling. I was happy to have them here, as was Jonathon, but it caused me to doubt myself and my ability to parent a little bit. On Sunday, Jonathon continued to test us constantly. He surely felt my lack of resolution on Saturday, and that, coupled with all the excitement of the weekend, gave him a sense of control over the environment. Not good.

Today Jonathon was pretty tough at therapy, and his resistance was at a level I have not seen in a couple of weeks. We are certainly noticing a bit of regression, but we know to expect that after seeing improvement. Jonathon seems to be a "textbook case", if there is such a thing, of attachment disorder.

Your email to us this morning was great. Paul read it, and said, "Michael might as well have been here. He knew EXACTLY what was going on." I think it reassured Paul to realize that these ups and downs are expected, and not something to panic about.

When our social worker arrived for the party on Saturday, she brought two boxes of Jonathon's belongings. On the top of one of the boxes was Jonathon's baby plate—a special little plate, which says "Baby's First Plate" on it. It's the kind a mommy gets for her son, and cherishes forever (assuming, of course, that she cherishes her son). It broke my heart to see this plate. A child should not be followed from home to home by his special baby plate! It was impossible for me to shake the feeling of mourning that I felt for him. I just wanted to scoop him up, run away to a very safe place, and protect him there, forever. No one should ever hurt him again. (On the other hand, he thinks I am hurting him when I do the very things that I must do to help him. He hates the holding, the control that he has lost. But I know that what I am doing is for his ultimate good, so I can keep going.)

Tonight Jonathon was very cuddly, and he is sleeping with one of my shirts that he loves. Hopefully we will have a happy day tomorrow.

Lori

March 27, 2001

Dear Lori,

Oh, my, do I ever know what you mean about not feeling—in front of all the observers and The Law—as if you could do for Jonathon what he needed on Saturday. You were on display, whether you wanted to be or not, and probably felt it. Jonathon had it in his hands to make it come out any way he wished (very frightening for him, and humiliating/disempowering for you).

A parent once told me she thought about writing some things about her son and the special way she needed to handle him on a card, laminating it, keeping it in her wallet, and having it ready to hand out at the grocery store or in front of extended family or others, in a pinch! She thought it would save her all the explanations, all the justifying, and let her focus on her child with RAD. Interesting thought, eh?

I'm amazed at your awareness that Jonathon could perceive your "lack of resolution" (on Saturday) and that that worried/frightened him. It is a source of never-ending irony and curiosity, isn't it, that a child who so fights for control (with every means at his disposal) could also so hunger to have someone else (who is sturdy, of course) take over?

I had dinner out with one of my grown sons last night. It is unusual for me to be away at dinnertime, but Mary and I were both surprised that this seemed to give both of the kids license to run all over her before and during dinner. I don't think we have realized how much they yearn for structure, yet how ready they are to leap at an opportunity for chaos, once the assurance of structure is missing.

Anyway, congratulations on getting through (sometimes that's the name of "success", isn't it: just "getting through"?) the weekend. It had all the ingredients for a full-scale meltdown, with threats of physical harm, and Jonathon being unable to come back to earth. That didn't happen.

My best,
Michael

March 27, 2001

Michael,

I just finished a long session of holding my precious son, who continues to fight so hard for control. A funny thought came to mind as we struggled. I had just finished (maybe an hour ago) reading your last email, about the mother who wants to laminate some information about the way she needs to handle her son on a card. (That way she could hand it out to the observing crowds during one of the many needed interventions on any given day.) I thought about that as I swept Jonathon up onto my lap, controlled his legs with mine, put one of his arms behind my back, held the other arm with mine, and cradled his head far enough from my chest to avoid his teeth. I was trying to figure out how, at that particular moment, I would reach into my wallet and pull out a laminated card. I think I had two toes which were not heavily involved in our struggle, but do not think they would have been much help. Possibly we should advertise our methods on a t-shirt, and wear it whenever we are out with our RAD children. Otherwise, by the time we have the child under enough control to be able to have a hand free to get to our wallet, the crowd has either gone away to mind their own business or to call the police and report possible abduction/abuse. I can hear it now: "Hello, police. You are needed immediately at the local grocery store. Some white lady is abusing an adorable little black boy. He clearly does not belong to her, by the way he is struggling. Please come right away. Bring a straight-jacket for the woman. She must be crazy."

What do you think? Does the t-shirt idea hold merit?

I have finished reading *Real Boys,* by William Pollock (which is much needed in today's society, but it should be common sense) and Daniel Hughes' *Building the Bonds of Attachment,* which gave me wonderful hope, ideas and, in general, rejuvenated me. It is a must-read book for anyone new to parenting one of our special RAD types. I just picked up *Handbook for Treatment of Attachment-Trauma Problems in Children* by Beverly James.

I will be working on t-shirt designs.
Lori

March 28, 2001

Dear Lori,

I'm afraid the message would have to be on the back of the t-shirt, as the front would be obscured by the whirling dervish.

Are you always this funny? Must help, some days. I have a little shortage in that department. Perhaps 33 years of this sort of trauma work has taken something out of me. Not hope, I know… but, maybe, some spontaneity.

We invited Beverly James to the Institute a few years back, as part of a series of seminars we sponsored on RAD treatment approaches. As you probably know, she is death on holding/attachment therapy. She is also a marvelous person and a good clinician.

As you undoubtedly know, many parents in your position have gone through the visual imagery of being arrested for what it looks as if they are doing "to" their child, in public. It's not a pretty sight, is it? Requires a greater capacity than many people have to stay focused (on what the child needs, instead of on what people are thinking), to remember what is important, to somehow avoid acute embarrassment. "Who needs it?", say some. Like a cop trying to wave his badge in the middle of the pandemonium, trying to "prove" he is there legitimately, and doing a legitimate thing. At some point, he even feels a little like a bad guy, as he tries to not get arrested right along with the criminal. At least those of us who have gone through it come out, at the other end, quite unable to quickly judge others.

Michael

March 29, 2001

Michael,

We might even need to print the words sideways on the t-shirt. I often find myself lying on my side to gain control of my special little darling. I never start out intending to lie on my side, but somehow end up there at some point in the struggle. I think I might need to learn some wrestling moves.

Last night Paul, his step-mom, and I went out to eat. We left the children home, with Rebecca (16) and Patrick (13) babysitting. When we called the kids to check on them, they said these very words: "Don't worry, everything is under control. Rebecca and Patrick are doing 'holding' with Jonathon because he hit the dog and tried to choke her. He is screaming, but we aren't letting it bother us. Have a good time!" Rebecca and Patrick actually did a great job of keeping everyone safe and sound. They are very special siblings.

Lori

March 29, 2001

Michael,

I started this e-mail last night, and somehow got sidetracked. Something to do with children and bedtime, I am sure. So tonight I will try again!

Jonathon and I went to therapy today, and had an interesting conversation on the way home. Jonathon told me that he wants to call his last parents and tell them he forgives them, and he wants them to forgive him, too. He wants to know if they might still love him, and thinks that they are missing him.

These comments came from out of the blue. There was no mention of this family in therapy today, and Jonathon has not mentioned them in days. I was very surprised when he initiated this conversation. My heart continues to break for this special little boy, every day. What an awful lot

of confusion and mixed messages he has to overcome. How horrible to think he might have been
loved, and then was given away. Not only has he had
lots of different parents, but lots of different homes,
beds, toys, clothes, pets…

Have you heard of Hope for the Children, the
foster care community in Illinois? I have a vision to
someday have such a community here, with all the
resources built in to the community that parents and
children need to survive the transitions from the
past, and to gain permanence for the future. The
supportive structure of the community is so helpful,
while parenting the most difficult children.

One of my older children is having a difficult
time with depression right now. We had a heart-to-
heart talk last night, and I asked if having Jonathon
in the home was adding to the depression. I was very
proud of my child's response. "Mom, I love
Jonathon. I know he takes a lot of your time, but
that is okay. Please do not do anything that will
destroy my life or his. He is my brother forever, and
I want him to be."

Jonathon wants me to hug him, so I will send this as is.

Lori

April 2, 2001

Michael,

Did you once tell me that very few families could
face a child like Jonathon and survive? We are currently facing destruction on too many fronts, and I
am really scared! I think each of us is holding on for
dear life, but am not sure if we are holding on to the
same lifeboat. You know the feeling you have when

"Did you once tell me that very few families could face a child like Jonathon and survive? We are currently facing destruction on many fronts, and I am really scared."

on a wild ride at an amusement park? The first time through, you have no idea what to expect next. You can be relatively certain that the outcome will be okay, because other people have taken the ride and survived. It is much easier to be confident the second time, though, once you have actually survived it, yourself. My tendency is to believe that our lives will turn out okay, and that we will come to the end of this horrible ride with everyone intact. But this is life, not a ride, and I have no guarantee of the outcome. (We once had a foster child with leukemia, and the outcome was not the one I wanted. Not even close.) So we hold on, we pray, we work at it as hard as we can…

Here is what the last two weeks have looked like: Jonathon was making terrific progress, and Paul was happy to let me know that he felt 95% certain that we would move into adoption with Jonathon. Jonathon clearly sensed this and moved into sabotage mode. He responds beautifully to Rebecca, pretty well to me, and absolutely defies anything that Paul tells him. Paul is the first dad (other than the one he had for nine months, in a foster home two placements ago) that Jonathon has had. Mostly he has had moms. That probably plays a role in Jonathon's response. Paul is now very frustrated, although he has been pretty successful in keeping a good attitude while working with Jonathon.

In the meantime, another child in our family has been diagnosed with depression, and started seeing a therapist. In the past month, things worsened for her, and she started seeing a psychiatrist. Depression runs in the family, and we saw the signs very clearly. The diagnosis was not a huge surprise. Medication was prescribed, and we are waiting for it to take effect. We are watching her 24 hours a day. For the next few weeks, I am doing a lot of reading, talking, hugging… .It is a very hard time. It is draining all of us, and wearing Paul down so much that he is not sure if he has anything to give to anyone else.

Paul's step mom and brother were here last week. We had a wonderful visit, but it meant that the routine was broken. I am sure that added to Jonathon's ability to cope. All of this chaos, added together, has our family reeling, and I am doing my best to try to get us all unified as we deal with each other. It has not been fun.

It is time for me to take Jonathon to therapy, and then come home to take my depressed child to therapy. I am going out for coffee with Lindsay tomorrow night for my therapy.

I hope to have some positive things to say when I write next, but felt it was important to share our very low time right now. I know that you know what I am talking about, and it helps so much to know that you (and others like you) have gone through some of these same things. You seem relatively sane, so there must be hope! (I can still laugh and joke a bit, so there IS hope.)

Off to therapy we go…

Lori

April 4, 2001

Dear Lori,

I've been traveling (this time to Toronto) again, and just got your last message.

Yes, I did say that: Very few families could face a child like Jonathon every day, and survive. That which pops up as a symptom of the pain varies a bit, from family to family: the parents' lovemaking with each other; another child's school work or behavior (everything from manners going to pot to an uncharacteristic report of aggression on the playground or hiding in the bedroom) or sanity; the identified child becoming an angel, but beginning to "divide and conquer" with respect to the two parents, or between a parent and another child; the family becoming reclusive. No one can weather a near-continuous storm without something getting pinched.

This is not to say that all is lost when something gets pinched. It is to say that the natural order of the universe is that something has to give at one end, when the other end is being squeezed so severely. Maybe it will become so overwhelming that you need to stop the storm, and Jonathon will have to go. Maybe the storm will let up from time to time, and light peeks through and you breathe deeply and go on (which means: get ready for the next storm, a little less depleted, and a little more able to weather it). Maybe you will decide the family cannot take so many hits, and Jonathon has to go. Or maybe you will decide that such "hits" are survivable, and that they—in some way you are not so sure of, at the moment—add to everyone's development or abilities or character or life story.

I am glad for you to tell me about such low times as you have recently had, and hope you are never ashamed of them.

What a powerful statement: "This is life, not a ride." The stakes are pretty high, aren't they? And I see the exquisite sensitivity you and Paul have to the height of those stakes. Nothing about this statement leads to a definitive "solution", does it? It just means it is all BIG.

Would you permit me to comment on a couple of things you said, even though it's not my business to do so?

A. That Jonathon's routine was disrupted by the visit of Paul's step mom is extremely important. It's a hard thing to remember, particularly when the child seems to do well with the disruption, at the time, and seems to be enjoying himself. Nonetheless, a price will almost always be paid. (This is not to say that disruptions should be avoided, just to avoid paying the price, by the way.)

B. In your March 29 message, you spoke of your wonder about whether Jonathon's presence was adding to the depression of one of your older children. You said the child responded, when asked about this, that she loved Jonathon, and went on to testify more about his importance in the family. While by no means am I suggesting that Jonathon plays a causal role in this depression, I believe it is important to remember that these are not mutually exclusive categories: A child can love a sibling deeply, and still be profoundly affected by that child's presence in the family. Guilt may preclude a child from acknowledging that, right along with the love, there is a co-existing resentment, sadness or even rage. They can BOTH be there, and this is something that most kids don't understand very well—as a result of which, they usually deny the less-socially-acceptable feeling, and express the "nicer" one.

C. I was amazed at the description of the kids doing holding with Jonathon. Goodness, they have learned a great deal from this experience, haven't they?

D. What a marvelous conversation about Jonathon's last parents! I wonder what, in his experience with you, has made that bubble to the surface? By the way, such thoughts—positive as they were—may have also laid the foundation for him to then come unraveled, later.

E. I am so sorry about your child with depression. This must weigh heavily on your heart, and further command your resources. While I do not know her at all, of course, and have no business, therefore, commenting on her, I have to say that I am impressed that she is making sure to get what she needs. And it appears it's working: she is home from school, getting lots of touch and emotional attention.

F. Are you the family cheerleader/spiritual uplifter at times like this?

Yes, I do know about Hope for the Children. It was started by a colleague, Brenda Krause Eheart, in a little town just up the road (Rantoul), on an abandoned Air Force base. They're doing good work. I heard from a place in Washington (state) who is starting something similar. (They wanted to use part of my film, "Multiple Transitions" for a fund-raising benefit, to support the new community for children project.)

The story continues... .
Michael

April 6, 2001

Michael,

We are still under siege in the Thomas household. Jonathon continues to defy Paul at every turn, which is extremely frustrating. Intellectually, we know that this behavior is not unexpected. Jonathon is clearly trying to get Paul to be the one to reject him, and is doing a great job of it. No matter how well we understand the reasons for his behavior, it is not easy to live with it. Paul has mentioned to me (more than once) that he is very willing to give Jonathon a chance (many chances) but that Paul is not willing to live like this forever. Understandable. Clearly some progress out of this current defiant stage is needed in order for Paul to feel comfortable signing on the dotted line and making Jonathon his son forever.

I hate being a foster mother to Jonathon. I compare foster parenting to a couple living together, and adoption to marriage. It is so easy to give up on someone when there is no lifetime commitment.

Now I find myself the foster mom to an extremely difficult child. I want to be his mom. I want to be forced to work through the hard times, with no thought of any options. I love working with Jonathon, and I love Jonathon. I know he is making progress, and that a lot more progress is just around the corner. But I do not know how far away we are from that corner, and I worry about how much stamina my family has, as we try to get there. I love my family: each of them as individuals, and all of us as a team. We need to stay intact. Can we do that, and get where we need to get with Jonathon? I really think so, but I just don't know for sure. For now, I guess I have to take things one day at a time. But I will give each day every ounce of energy that I have, and I will not give up unless forced to do so. I pray that day never comes.

Michael, do you know how much we appreciate your insights, and the time you spend corresponding with us? One of the reasons that I think we will make it is that we have such wonderful resources to draw from. We have you, and Jon-the-therapist (who is absolutely wonderful), and books and websites. We have supportive friends and supportive extended family (only some of whom think we are crazy). We have a strong faith in God. We will survive this. The final outcome is not something I can predict with 100% certainty. Will we adopt Jonathon, will he remain with us as a foster child, or will he move on? I know what I hope for, but have no guarantee. I do know that we will all learn and grow. Maybe we will even look back on this time fondly, from some point in the distant future.

Let me comment on some of your comments:

A. We do understand that each disruption in our "normal" routine throws Jonathon off, and that a price is paid each time. It is such a fine line to walk, trying to decide how much disruption is okay. For instance, another of Paul's brothers will be here next Wednesday for a visit. He is bringing his oldest daughter, who is close to Rebecca's age, with him. We always love to see them, and are excited about the opportunity for them to meet Jonathon. I know that the visit will throw Jonathon off a bit, but feel that it is worth it for him to have a chance to get to know the extended family and get a sense of belonging to them all. I have no problem with these visits. I do, however, plan to think twice before planning any large parties in the near future. I also limit how often I take Jonathon out, and the places that I take him. I want him to experience success as often as possible. I do not plan to enroll him in school for at least a year or two. I will home-school him, again allowing him a chance for success. He does not need to be thrown back into large groups, over-stimulated, and then forced into bad behavior and meltdowns. I want to limit his opportunities for failure.

B. My child who is experiencing depression is an extremely wonderful nurturer, a caregiver kind of person. I know that she truly loves Jonathon, and that she would be very upset if anything caused the placement in our home to disrupt.

C. We have been amazed by many things our children have done over the years. They played a big role in James' therapy when he first came to us, and have helped in so many ways with so many different children. I remember once, when Rebecca was 12, that we had a foster baby. This baby was up a lot at night, and after about 3 months I was worn out. One night I noticed that the baby bed was in Rebecca's room. She announced that she was going to do the night feedings that night so that I could get some sleep!

D. I am wondering, in reference to Jonathon's conversation with me about forgiving his last parents, if the fact that we have a positive and ongoing relationship with another of his former foster families has had an effect on Jonathon's desire to re-establish a relationship with his last parents. He was with the family with whom he still has contact, then the adoptive home, before coming to us. Could he be wondering why we leave that gap in the middle, between two families that are currently involved with him?

E. Yes, I do tend to be the family cheerleader/spiritual uplifter when times are tough. I know the importance of working as a team, and of trying to see the big picture. On the other hand, I have a very supportive, easy-to-work-with team. Makes my job pretty delightful.

Our goals are:

1. to continue growing as individuals in this family;
2. to grow and strengthen our family unit;
3. to successfully help Jonathon to attach, preferably with us;
4. to start a community, similar to Hope for the Children, here in the D.C. area. We really need that kind of help for the number of needy, hard-to-place children we have here.

I think that is all the thinking I can do for tonight.
Lori

April 6, 2001

Dear Lori,

I'm curious about Jonathon's challenging Paul so much. Here's a phenomenon I've seen in clinical practice with certain kids, offered to you not because I think it's what is happening in your house (I couldn't possibly know), but only to mull over: A child with great anger overflows with impulses (to hit, to run away, to bite others or himself, to steal, just to rage). He wishes he were not filled up with these feelings, these urges, but he is. He wishes for a power great enough to control the impulses. Certainly this power is not inside of him. He does not ask for help with the impulses, of course, because he does not wish to acknowledge vulnerability. So he begins provoking the largest power source he sees in the family, hoping to get the person with this power to use his/her power to align with the child against that child's own impulses. In plain terms: the child looks for help against himself—more to the point, against that part of himself that he cannot control. Externalizing this part of himself helps to identify the "enemy" more clearly. Then he tickles the tail of a dragon in the family, trying to get someone to vanquish the "foe".

It's an amazingly clever (and often very effective) way to deal with the sheer volume and force of all that goes on (and goes OFF!) inside the child. It's just possible that Jonathon needs Paul's power. Just a thought...

My best... Michael

April 8, 2001

Michael,

Your comments about children like Jonathon who need a strong someone on their side, to help them fight the part of them that they cannot control, makes a lot of sense. Paul and I discussed this possibility at length, and both think we might see signs that that is exactly what is going on with Jonathon.

Paul has noted some interesting things with Jonathon this week. He has found that Jonathon responds to him better when he calls Jonathon "Johnny". He uses the name endearingly, and Jonathon has tuned in to him each time he uses that name.

Tonight Jonathon said something that was rude, and then held out his hand to me. He said: "Please hit my hand. I get better when you hit my hand." He was asking for help controlling himself. (We do not hit his hand, or any other part of his body, so this request baffled me.) My response to his request was to scoop him up, hold him in a tight hug, and tell him nice things to say. Then he got lots of tickles.

Jonathon has started doing a lot of name-calling and rude talking ("stupid idiot", and the like). He always apologizes immediately, but then repeats the words minutes later. The apologies seem a bit like manipulation—very straightforward and with little feeling. I think Jonathon is just doing what he knows he will need to do (with the apology) in order to avoid trouble.

This morning Jonathon went to the gym with Paul. He often gives Paul a rough time when it is time to leave. Today, however, Paul was in for a happy surprise when he went in to the children's' room to get Jonathon. Jonathon ran up to him and was very animated. He told Paul that they were watching a movie named "Beethoven". He excitedly told Paul the whole plot and was very happy to do so. Then he asked Paul to watch it for a few minutes with him. Paul sat down with him for five minutes to watch the movie, and Jonathon was satisfied. Paul told Jonathon when the five minutes were up, and Jonathon left with Paul with no complaint. Paul was very encouraged by this episode.

All in all, today (Saturday) was an excellent day. Typically, Saturdays have been one of our worst days (lack of normal routine, and all that). But today was great.

We will continue to do what we can. Hope it is enough...
Lori

April 8, 2001

Dear Lori,

"Beethoven": a movie about a big, not-too-attractive, klutzy creature that tries to fit into a family and keeps messing up, and they like him and keep him, anyway.

Michael

April 8, 2001

Michael,

Why is it that I get sooo excited about things with Jonathon that would seem so ordinary with my other children? Something happened tonight that thrilled me, but it might not mean much to most moms and dads out there. I know that you will understand my excitement, though.

I teach a class at my church on Sunday nights, and Jonathon and James are both in it. Jonathon's behavior was not the best tonight. He was very good in our group game-time, but not well-behaved most of the rest of the night. As we were driving home, he asked me if I was going to tell Dad that he did not behave well. Here is how the conversation went:

"Mom, do you have to tell Dad that I was bad at church? Could you tell him that I was good the whole time?" Jonathon's voice had his best kitten-like quality. (Jonathon often takes on the sounds and voices of animals. He has a kitten, a dog, and a little mouse. Sometimes he is a lion. The sounds are distinct.)

"Jonathon, I never lie to Dad. What do you think I should tell him?" I was interested to see what he would say.

"Well, you could just tell him about the good stuff, and not tell him about the bad stuff." There was a bit of a plea in Jonathon's voice.

"I'll tell you what, Jonathon. I am going to let you decide what to tell Dad. You can tell him anything you want, as long as it is the truth. You decide."

We drove up to the house, and Paul was outside taking our trash out to the curb. Jonathon jumped out of the car, and excitedly told Paul: "Dad, I was really good at game-time. I was really good." Pause. "But I didn't stay in line. I was good most of the time, but I got out of line."

I was thrilled! I gave Jonathon permission to leave out anything, as long as what he told was the truth. His conscience would not let him deceive his dad. He spilled the beans on himself because he could not lie to his dad's face.

Don't get me wrong. Jonathon is very good at lying, and does so frequently. But tonight, on this one occasion, he could not do it. He freely offered the truth!

Could we be making progress?

Interesting stuff with our youngest this weekend! Just when we start to despair, a ray of sunshine breaks through.

Lori

April 10, 2001

Dear Lori,

You and Paul ought to have your brains and your instincts preserved for all eternity, after you depart.

What a great comeback. A perfect development-enhancing ploy: presume a solid interior life (conscience, morality), then place confidence in him to explore it (inside himSELF) and then let it lead him. He got nearly everything he wanted, but he also had to sit with the responsibility.

Michael

April 12, 2001

Michael,

Paul started reading *Building the Bonds of Attachment,* and is inspired by it. I think that reading it when I did (just as I was beginning to try my hand at parenting a child with attachment disorder) was vital to my ability to keep "The Attitude" up and the frustration down. I am thrilled that Paul is reading it.

I have started reading Beverly James, and am intrigued by the theories of attachment. Paul and I learn from others, learn from our mistakes, and learn from our successes. But learn we must, because a little boy's future depends on it. The stakes are so high, and this same story is being played out in so many lives all over the world. It is overwhelming to think about.

In chapter one [of Beverly James] she talks about the consequence of trauma, and persistent fear is listed. Do you think persistent fear includes phobias? Jonathon is clearly bug-phobic. It is going to be a long spring and summer. Anything that flies, crawls, or has any insect qualities sends him into panic. He runs to me screaming. I am torn between being Jonathon's protector and trying to rationalize with him. I am choosing more of a protector role, while still trying to explain to him that the little critters will not do him much harm. I wonder if this is really a phobia for Jonathon, or if he has a huge need to create opportunities for someone to protect him. Maybe both.

I loved your analysis of the movie "Beethoven" and what it might mean to Jonathon. I had not given a bit of thought to the content of the movie, and laughed when I read your email.

Lori

April 12, 2001

Dear Lori,

I was about to answer in the negative to your question about fear and phobias. Children with RAD often have extraordinarily strange fears—made more strange by their mixture with absolute fearlessness. The creepy-crawly (particularly flying bugs) panic reaction is very common in children with the sort of background Jonathon has. My stepson, Jeremy, runs screaming when a bee is near but would, I suspect, approach a hippopotamus in the driveway with curiosity and interest. I feel certain this is principally about such children as Jeremy and Jonathon despising surprise and loss of control. (I know I need say not one word more about either of these issues to you, as you seem to understand them so well, with respect to Jonathon.) So these are not standard fears, and they are not trauma-based fears (in the classical sense of being connected with a traumatic experience with the feared object). That pretty much makes them phobic reactions, then, so I must revise my first reaction and say that you are probably right. They have obsessive qualities, they are not realistic, and the children having them do not realistically appraise the capacity of the feared object to cause pain or damage. Instead, the feared object evokes fear because the feared object (fly, mosquito, bee, spider) threatens to overwhelm, overtake, and, therefore, take control. The child cannot manage the anxiety fast enough. Jeremy, at least, has to flee—shriek, get up and run, and tell me.

My rather dopey reaction is try to reassure, with a realistic appraisal of the actual danger of the bee. This has never done a great deal of good. However, I suspect that my calm voice and demeanor WHILE I am being unhelpfully rational DOES help, by introducing the option (through modeling, not telling) of being calm and in control. After a few thousand episodes, I suspect some of this will rub off. (But, then, again, who knows?!)

Odd to see a dictator crumble at the feet of a fly, isn't it?
Michael

April 13, 2001

Michael,

We currently have some visitors. Jonathon is enjoying the extra attention and only needs to be held slightly more than usual (so far, anyway; perhaps I have probably just doomed myself by making such a claim).

I can't tell you how helpful it is to have our journal of correspondence. We refer to it when we share about Jonathon with family members who do not understand our new child and what we are trying to do with him. Preserving the memories correctly would not be possible without a journal. There is just too much going on today to be able to keep accurate track of yesterday. I really need to look back on it frequently in order to see some hope of progress and to have, therefore, the energy to proceed.

Jonathon is becoming such a member of the family. Yesterday with all of the children in the van, James was trying to say something to Rachael. James can be very hard (actually impossible, sometimes) to understand. Rachael was not understanding him. Just as I was about to speak up with a translation, Jonathon beat me to it! He said: "James is trying to say… " I was shocked (and touched) that Jonathon had accurately translated for James, and I asked him how he knew what James was saying. "It's easy, Mom. James is my bwatha." It was a priceless moment! Such an innocent little exchange, with such profound meaning!

Lori

April 16, 2001

Michael,

We watched out the window, tonight, as Jonathon and James played outside together, giggling and romping. It was very moving for me. Jonathon and James are good for each other. James is more animated than ever before. Jonathon has forced him to reach deep inside himself and come out of his shell a bit. And Jonathon is playing with, and sometimes being protective of, James. Jonathon is learning to care about someone his own age: his best buddy, as he calls him.

I have been doing a lot of thinking in my free time. I used to do some speaking to women's' groups, and some of my talks came back to me in bits and pieces. One of my favorite sayings, in reference to our faith in God, is the "Three T's of Faith": Turn, Trust, and Triumph. The Three T's work for attachment, too. If I can get my child to turn to me, to run to me when in need, to talk to me instead of keeping things in, then we have a good basis to start our work together. If I respond well to his needs, and he is capable of beginning to trust, then we have made a huge second step. Once that trust actually results in a positive, working attachment, we will triumph. So now I will remember my "Three T's of Attachment", and hope to achieve them.

Lori

April 16, 2001

Dear Lori,

A patient wrote a marvelous poem to me, some years ago, in which he described what therapy was like for him, suggested some ground rules, and asked for some compassion. Then he added a final stanza—evidently written several days after the main part of the poem, as a sort of afterthought—in which he mused about whether God was trying to do some work on ME (Michael), through him (the patient). He put it sort of amusingly ("... wouldn't it be just like God if He were... "), but it was also obvious that he was dead serious. And he finished with a barely-concealed challenge about how old wineskins would burst when filled with new wine, so that a paradigm shift might have to occur.

I was blown away. That notion has come back to me often, since then: How can I know what is really going on? How can I know what is supposed to happen? As Jonathon is causing people such distress that they must question much about themselves, wouldn't it be just like God to have dumped him here in the first place to do a work on James—and our job is just to hang on, to cooperate and not get in the way (but not to "cure" Jonathon, as long as he's here, because that's not what God's main point is). Exhausting, yet invigorating thoughts...

Michael

April 16, 2001

Michael,

I am confused about your last message, and would love to have you clarify the following:

"Wouldn't it be just like God to have dumped him here in the first place to do a work on James—and our job is just to hang on, to cooperate and not get in the way (but not to 'cure' Jonathon, as long as he's here, because that's not what God's main point is)."

You don't think that is part of our thought process, do you? I have to admit that when I first read your email, my mother bear instincts came out. I was troubled, to put it mildly. I truly believe that Jonathon is here for Jonathon's sake. But I get ahead of myself. I will write more after I understand your message better.

Lori

April 17, 2001

Dear Lori,

Experience teaches me that carrying on a long-distance conversation about highly value-laden, intensely personal stuff is, to say the least, fraught with danger. True understanding/communication is not terribly likely, and hurt is.

But I certainly won't duck your questions, nor look aside from the evocation of your mother bear.

No, I was not reporting on what I imagined your framing of Jonathon's purpose on this planet was/is. I was only saying that I have been stunned, over and over in my life, with how little I know about what is REALLY going on, or what is ALSO going on. Sometimes, years later, it appears there were purposes that none of us could possibly have grasped at the moment. Even for those who don't believe that life is purposeful, they may be forced to admit that, at the least, the effects of some event or some person in their lives was altogether unanticipated.

So your observations about the wonder of James and Jonathon together merely made me think of my patient's poem, and how captured I was by the notion that he may have been in MY life for a reason, every bit as much as my having been in HIS for a reason. This didn't mean that his only purpose on this planet was to have an effect on me, of course. Of course, Jonathon is Jonathon. But can we know why he is as sick as he is, or why he is sick just exactly the WAY he is, or how he will get well, or when, or who he will touch along the way, and what astonishing higher purposes will be served en route? How did he end up with the Thomas family, REALLY? Was he needed there, by someone? And does being so needed take away from his selfhood?

Michael

April 17, 2001

Michael,

I am truly thrilled and relieved by your response. Before I explain, let me say that I am pleased that you responded at all. You have been so good to help encourage and educate us in this process, and I almost bit the very hand that is helping to feed us. Thank you for your patience.

I agree with you 100% that there are multiple purposes for many of the perplexing events in our lives. Renee's life was a short one, but God placed her with us because He knew we would love her and care for her, AND He knew that we would be touched and forever changed by her presence in our lives. I DO see that in Jonathon's placement. We all have so much to gain and learn by having him with us. The part that gave me cause for concern was the, "... but not to cure Jonathon, as long as he's here... " Everything in me wants to help him in any way I can, and I feel strongly that his main purpose here is for his own good. That we need him is a given. But I do not want to adopt him because we need, and are blessed by, his presence. I want to adopt him because I love him, and want his needs met. If this placement were not in his best interest, I would want him to move along. I really feel that this is the best place for him. We love him tremendously, and I will do anything in my power to nurture and love him.

Clearly, attachment therapy works—at least for the parent! I am attached. I don't know about Jonathon, but Jon's methods have gotten the best of me. My objective, foster mother mentality flew way out the window and has not been seen in ages. (Please understand that I know there is a wonderful service being done by foster parents, and that I do know how to be a good one when necessary. I have fostered, loved, and released many children. I am not knocking foster parents. I am one. Just not with this kid! I no longer want to be anything but "mommy" to him.)

It is incredible to watch life unfold, and realize how little I know about what I am doing today, or will be doing tomorrow. Without a faith in God, and the knowledge that He does have a plan, how could I keep going?

Lori

April 19, 2001

Michael,

Did you know that if you are typing a message, and a dog comes along and rests his chin on the "escape" button, the message disappears? I have written this message to you twice this morning and, just as I make some progress in my writing, Luka comes along to "help". Luka is a yellow lab, belonging to our friend Siobhan, who is here for doggy-daycare (Luka, that is, not Siobhan). So here goes my third try.

A clearer picture of Jonathon has begun to emerge, for me, as I participate in a Bible study. We had a debate on relationship vs. rules, and I wrote this.

Jonathon, in his previous family, exhibited much defiant behavior and no respect for any rules. The family wanted to help him learn, and their motives were probably good. Their response to him, however, seemed to be lacking what he needed. As he disobeyed, they added more rules and more structure in order to force him into compliance. The more he resisted, the more structure was added. Unfortunately, the structure did not include holding, closeness. In the end, he was in lots of therapy, a rigid full-day school setting, and little else. Their methods of discipline were probably the same as those that many of us have used with many of our "normal" children. Jonathon did not respond.

Jonathon, in his defiance, was able to reproduce the chaos and lack of bonding that he was used to. He did not have to change, because he was able to make his environment one that worked for him as he was.

The rules had no impact on Jonathon. They did not fit into his perception of the world. By not following them, he was able to get a lot of attention and keep things the way he knew them to be.

Jonathon really needed to learn to build a relationship in order to change his point of reference. He is now learning, slowly, how to bond. We are seeing progress. As we see a relationship increase, we see his desire to defy us decrease.

Therefore, a relationship results in a desire to follow the rules (at least, to some degree). As a Christian, I want to follow the rules that God has put in place because I have a desire to please Him, I know that He has my best interests in mind, and I trust Him. My children, hopefully, know that our rules are made in their best interests, and they trust us. They have a relationship with us that means that (sometimes, anyway) they willingly follow our rules. We hope to help Jonathon build a relationship and a trust that allows him to be able to also follow rules a bit more willingly. All of this is to say that rules are vital for our survival, but that a relationship with the rule-maker helps in our ability and desire to follow the rules.

We are moving forward into adoption with Jonathon, and he senses it. How is it that these little ones are sooooo perceptive? A few weeks ago, when Paul felt that we might want to consider the "adoption thing", Jonathon responded with some terrible behavior—bad enough that Paul felt a need to pull back and regroup. Now that we feel ready to move forward, and discussed it with our oldest children yesterday, you can imagine how Jonathon is acting. No one has said anything to him about adoption, but he must sense it. He is trying his hardest to get us to pull back again. This time we anticipated his defiance, and are actually amused at his attempts to manipulate the course of events.

We have seen that Jonathon has the potential to bond, and that some first steps have been made. His affect is so much more relaxed. He responds to emotion and affection. He smiles easily, laughs appropriately and, in general, is more responsive than before. We see hope.

Are we crazy to adopt, expecting that change will continue? I would never marry someone with hope that they would change. A marriage partner should be someone with whom you can live as they currently are. But our job as parents is to create change in our children. Not change in who they are, but in how they respond to the world. The baby stage is cute, but a good parent helps the child move out of that stage and into the next. So I guess it is fair to say that we can love this child, adopt him, and still expect to help him to change in order to better survive this world. I know that his potential for change, given his special needs and background, is not the same as that of a "normal" child. But whatever Jonathon's potential, I think it will be best reached if he is in our family.

Lori

April 20, 2001

Dear Lori,

Yes, of course you are crazy.

Just kidding. Well, actually, not entirely kidding. Who else, except a crazy person, would invite the hurricane into the living room, believing— on faith, mostly—that there is something amazing at the center of a hurricane, that the calm after the hurricane is especially sweet and the air sometimes smells good, and that it's usually true that there will not be another hurricane fast on the heels of the one you just invited in? WHO DOES THIS?! Who is so nutty (or arrogant, or deranged, or faithful, or flush with hope) to imagine that the hurricane can be tamed before it destroys the house, and that some part of the hurricane will be left after that taming, so that it is worth the wind and the threat?

You peeked, of course. You have a hunch about what may lie inside there, at the center. And something about your makeup, your faith, your own lived experience suggests that you not only can, but should, hang on, reach deeper, reach out, and do the ridiculous/impossible/disruptive/humane thing.

Amazing that Jonathon knows, and I don't doubt you for one moment that he does. How can a child smell safety-that-is-actually-dangerous from 50 paces? Cool that you anticipated it, second time around, and disarmed the power of his reactive behavior by getting there before he did.

Michael

April 25, 2001

Hi Michael,

We have decided, beyond the shadow of a doubt, to move into adoption. We are meeting with our social worker on May 3, to start the paperwork. We have seen that we really love Jonathon, and that we just can't ask him to ever move again. He is responding to therapy, so we have great hope for continued progress. Our communications a week or two ago, when I misunderstood something you said and my "mother-bear" instincts came out, helped us to see how very much we love this little guy and want what is best for him.

Interesting things are happening lately. It is funny to see that we can read something in print, and then forget to apply it to our lives when the need arises. I have read, in many places, not to overdo the praise when something goes well. On Sunday morning, Jonathon went to Sunday school, without a parent to stay with him, for the first time! He was very good, and the Sunday school teacher gave us a great report. We were soooo excited. Jonathon ran out of the class, yelling "Mom, Dad, I was very, really good." We SHOULD have said "Good job, Jonathon." Then a quick high-five, and on with our day. But NOOO. We made a huge deal about it. "Great job, Buddy! Mom and Dad are SO proud of you! We knew you could do it!!" High-five and hug from Mom. High-five and hug from Dad. We continued to talk about it, and brag about Jonathon to the other kids, as we walked out of that class. HOW STUPID! Can you imagine how Jonathon acted the rest of the day? About as bad as a child can act. Screaming, clinging, hitting, spinning more and more out of control.

I think two things contributed to his meltdown. One was the lavish praise we gave. He knew he could not maintain great behavior forever, and would, therefore, win our "disapproval" soon. He might as well do it in his own time. Also, I think that Jonathon's good behavior in class that morning probably took every ounce of emotional energy that he had. He gave it his all, and nothing was left to be utilized during the next few hours. Looking back, I would do two things differently. I would tone down the praise, and I would make our next activity very low-key, so that nothing was expected of him. Just a quiet hour playing outside, or reading together. Nothing taxing.

That is all I have for now. I am too tired from my day of parenting to have more on my mind than a thought or two.

Lori

April 25, 2001

Dear Lori,

Your consideration of Jonathon's—and your own—behavior last Sunday is worthy of a clinical paper, in its own right. I couldn't agree more with each part, tho' I was especially surprised to read of your awareness of how much energy it must have taken for him to hold it together in the morning (and how little he had left, then, for receiving your accolades, or for managing his subsequent behavior).

Such a balancing act is required, eh? And—as you have said so often—that which works like a charm with another child is not a predictably effective approach to take with Jonathon.

We had a touch-and-go experience of this kind with Jeremy, late last summer. He was not, at almost age 9, able to ride a bike. He barely managed on a tiny bike with training wheels. This was not fun. He was teased by other kids who saw him on "the baby bike", and he had it regularly confirmed for him, thereby, that he was different, and probably incompetent. I wondered, after watching him carefully for a few weeks, whether his fear was a little like his rage: both were things he needed/wanted help with (even as he would deny that he did, and act haughty about it). To leave him alone with either, I conjectured, was to abandon him. So I decided to press the case. I told him that he was able to ride a "big boy's bike", that I would help him with it and never leave his side until he said I could, but that I knew he could do it. He protested vociferously. I had no idea if I was right. For all I knew, he did have a mysterious motor problem that kept him from being able to balance a bike (the same motor problem that makes him walk on his toes, shuffle his feet persistently, be very clumsy throwing a ball, etc.?). Or, maybe fear (and, for all I knew, a good Latin-American terror of humiliation, a wounding of pride, that actually had little to do with his attachment disorder) was at the core. He wasn't able to tell me, and I didn't think I should leave him alone with whatever it was, so I pushed.

He was furious with me. He called me names. He refused. He screamed at me the whole time I ran alongside him, holding either him, or the seat. I told him, on Thursday, that on Saturday he would know how to do it. We decided (mostly, I decided) that we would find out if I was right at 10:00, after we had Saturday morning breakfast (a big deal in our house).

When the appointed hour arrived, we all gathered in the driveway. (Should this be a private thing? Or should everyone be available to share his triumph? Or was it going to be a public shame event?) He climbed on his brother's bike, I steadied him, and I ran alongside for 10 feet or so (while he berated me for doing everything wrong). Then he ordered me to get out of the way, and off he sailed.

He rode that stupid bike as if he had been secretly riding for years. His older sister watched, with her mouth hanging open. (She had stood by for years as he crashed, screamed, blamed everyone else, demanded the tiny bike with "baby wheels", etc.)

On Monday night, at supper, we presented him with a trophy with his name on it, and the words, "… For Courage", and a Dairy Queen cake. He kept rubbing his eyes (saying that he had something in them) and looking away. I think he was overcome.

We got lucky. For some reason, he could stand that much attention, that much implied demand (Will he always be able to ride, or will it all go away the next time he gets on the bike? Will he have courage about other things?) without a meltdown. No way would I recommend that much noise about accomplishment, normally (for all the reasons you described).

A week later, we followed through with our pledge to get him a new bike (if he mastered a big boy's bike). He showed not the slightest interest in it, and never said thank you. It took a few days, in fact, for him to even climb on it. He rides every day, now, however, and relishes my willingness to stretch the boundaries of his riding territory. He crashed the other day (interestingly, on his cousin's small bike—I don't believe he has ever crashed on his own, big-boy bike), and merely came to us for attention to the wound. Again (for reasons we are helpless to explain) there was no meltdown, no raging, no screaming from a block away that it was our fault.

Boy, do we ever learn by trial and error. And even that which works with one wounded child—whose life has been filled with loss and powerlessness—may be completely contraindicated with another, with similar wounds. Nobody can write a book about these kids, I am convinced. Each of us has to learn, and just share the principles—but not necessarily the strategies—with each other.

Michael

April 29, 2001

Michael,

The "crazy lying" has become a non-stop problem with Jonathon. He tells us he already put his bike away, and it is sitting in front of the house. He says that dad already gave him his medicine, and dad is just in the other room saying that he has not given it. It happens about twenty bazillion times a day. We are catching most of the lies, I think, and trying to work with him. Sometimes it is easy to find a good response. With the bike still outside, we tell him that he must be confused, because the bike is still outside where he left it earlier. We encourage him to go out and take care of it, because if he leaves it out, somebody might take it. We remind him that we will not buy a new one if he leaves it out and somebody takes it.

We plan to start adoption paperwork on Thursday, and with all the lying we are experiencing, Paul is wondering if we are doing the right thing. We can postpone the paperwork if we are not in complete agreement by Thursday. I want us to give our best to Jonathon, and we can't do that if we are not 100% sure. On the other hand, how many of us get cold feet before any big decision? I remember walking down the aisle and wondering if I knew what I was doing. Now, twenty-one years and six children later, I think I made a pretty good choice! Even so, I know that making a permanent commitment to Jonathon is a big decision and must be made carefully.

But how can one "carefully" take on a child like Jonathon? Any child brings some risk with him, and a hurt child surely brings more risk. Doesn't he also bring more hope? Hope that the world is still a good place? Hope that a hurt child can be loved and experience some level of healing? Hope that each of us can stretch ourselves more than we thought possible, and enjoy the process? Hope that God, in His big plan, knows what He is doing and brought Jonathon to us for a reason?

Lori

April 30, 2001

Dear Lori,

Boy, I don't envy you and Paul in a week like the one you were describing in your April 29 message: about to take a HUGE leap, and wondering exactly how one contorts one's body to jump. Is it a giant, joyous, expansive movement? (Who knows what you might hit in such a move?) Or is it a more constricted, wary movement? (So maybe you don't get all the way there in such a move?) Do you ask questions about the risks; if so, how do you know when you have enough information? I suppose you are past that time by now...

The crazy-lying matter can be SO depleting, can't it? Interesting that you took note of the cause-and-effect part of this problem. There is, in many kids with RAD, a true disorder relative to cause-and-effect, and I have always been suspicious about how big a part might be played by the child actually not GETTING IT, about how things connect. I acknowledge that it doesn't look this way, at the time. The child's lying is usually so bold and so outrageous as to be either laughable or worthy of a hanging, depending on one's mood at the moment. But the very ridiculousness of it does raise the specter that the child honestly doesn't see things the way the rest of us do. One thing we know from developmental neurology is that the combination of prenatal exposure to alcohol (perhaps other drugs, as well) and maternal stress seems to be a recipe for a processing disorder in the child that includes a breakdown in cause-and-effect linking. This is the same disorder that makes planning and anticipation such a challenge for some children. I would love to hear any more of your observations about this. I can tell you what you already know, probably: that consequences work about as well as righteous yelling about it— which is to say, not much.

My heart goes out to Paul, imagining how much he must be struggling with these decisions, and how much evolution has prepared him to ferociously fight to protect his family against anything that might hurt it, or destroy it, or even rock it too much. There must be days when Jonathon seems like just that sort of threat, and I GET IT about why he would feel blue, or frightened, or intensely wary (not things you have told me about his feelings right now—just things I am guessing). This is part of how a man loves his family.

Michael

chapter IV.

Looking Back...

A few notes about my feelings, as I review this manuscript
Lori Thomas

"Dreams for the future must be bigger

than memories from the past."

(Lori's pastor, James Ahlemann)

It is now 2004, and I am amazed, as I look back at this crucial decision-making period in our lives. Those first months were torture. A lack of direction, combined with a lack of trust on all sides—then further confounded by Jonathon's constantly-shifting but often very troubling behavior—caused us frustration and a constant need for reflection. During this time, I watched a video about the early English settlers at Jamestown. An analogy occurred to me. On one of the walls of the museum at Jamestown are the words, "...success of the Jamestown settlement was not inevitable".

From a perspective of more than 200 years in the future, I have the luxury of knowing that the colonies did grow, and they birthed a new nation that is now a major world power. But, at one point, when Jamestown dwindled down to 60 men and no food, their survival was not inevitable. It took the grace of God, some lucky breaks, some very hard work, and an incredible will to survive in order to have a positive outcome.

Despite hardship, discouragement and defeat, conditions in Jamestown stabilized. In time, the structure of the settlement matured, setting the pattern for generations to come. A working environment was birthed. It took time, but it took hold. Once in place, this working structure was something upon which the future could be based. Life could move forward. Once life began the forward motion, the settlement took off. In less than a generation, there was great prosperity and a good life in that colony. The hard work paid off.

What a great lesson to reflect upon, as we worked with Jonathon. Would the hard work pay off? Would a structure, a relationship, mature to the point that we could have a work that would endure? Only time would tell. There was no way to know the future, but we knew that it was time to get our family moving forward, and it was time to make hard decisions.

Back to our story...

chapter V.

The Letters: A Decision Is Made

"Without a vision, the people perish."
(One of Lori's favorite scriptures —Proverbs 29:18)

May 4, 2001

Michael,

Just a quick note to tell you that we did the big deed yesterday, and signed paperwork to start the adoption process of our Jonathon! We feel confident that it is the right thing to do, for all involved. We would have a hard time living with any other decision, which makes this decision the only one to make!

Our family was fine before Jonathon came along, and there was no hole that we were aware of. If we had never met Jonathon, we would not have known that we were not complete. However, we did meet Jonathon, and Jonathon clearly needed us. As life progressed with him in our home, (has it really only been four months?) we saw that we needed him, too. There is a side of him that has a lot of love and sweetness, and that side of him needs a chance to survive. We all (meaning him, our family, and our community) benefit from him finding his best and using it.

We told Jonathon the news at dinner last night. He smiled and looked pleased. There was no big deal made, just a happy announcement. It was interesting that Jonathon did not leave the table quickly. (He usually asks to be excused within a few minutes. He never stays through a whole meal.) Last night, Jonathon played with his food for a couple of minutes, and then came over and sat on my lap. He stayed as we all visited, and seemed very content. It was a precious moment!

We will not be surprised if he tries to sabotage the process, and will not panic if we see some regression. (I need to repeat that to myself three times to make it stick. It is easy to say those words now.)

We are happy. All of Jonathon's siblings are in happy agreement with our decision. Our extended family says they are, too. I think they are cautiously optimistic. Our friends are a mixed bag. Some of them are happy for us, some are praying for us, and some think we have gone completely crazy.

Jonathon's social worker is thrilled! Jon-the-wonderful-therapist is very happy for all of us, too.

A new chapter in the Thomas Family saga begins!
Lori

May 8, 2001

Dear Lori,

Oh, my! I'm sorry it took me so long to get to THIS message...
Congratulations to the planet, thanks be to God. Good things do happen. My prayers are, and will continue to be, with all of you.

Michael

May 9, 2001

Michael,

It feels so good to have the adoption decision behind us. My gut feeling is that having the "forever" mentality will help us make it through future trials. It is challenging to face big issues with a child and to have side issues (should we call the social worker and have him removed? how much more can we take?) also occupying the mind and depleting the energy. Now we can focus more clearly on the job ahead of us.

The "crazy lying" issue really intrigues me. I trust Jonathon's memory quite a bit. He recalls things from the past that are verifiable, and so far his memory seems very accurate. He remembers a car accident from when he was with his birth mom, at age 2. He remembers a lot about his time with at least one of the earlier foster families, and that mom has let me know that those are accurate memories. He remembers anything promised to him, very clearly! Therefore, faulty memory is ruled out as a cause. So here are the questions I ask myself: Does Jonathon think that we will believe his lies? Does he talk himself into believing the lies himself? Or is he aware that he is telling a "mistruth"? Is it a coping device, trying to keep out of trouble? Is it a survival technique, carried over from bad times in his past? Was lying vital in his past? Was he taught to lie? ("If the police come, hide in the closet and pretend we are not home.") Or is it simply another form of testing us, to see what we are made of, and what we will put up with? Is it a habit, done without giving it another thought? Or is it done with intention and forethought? I have theories, but want to really focus on each incident for a period of time, keep my mind open, and see what conclusions we can draw.

We are not labeling the lying as "bad", and do not have consequences attached to lying at this point. Instead, we are treating it as an "oops" kind of thing. "Oops, Jonathon, I think you made a mistake. You might have thought you put your bike in the garage, but let's take a look. Oh, my, there it is, on the sidewalk! How do you think it got there? What shall we do now?" Jon (as in Jon-the-wonderful-therapist) gave us some suggestions, which has led to an idea. We are considering a "lying day". Everything told that day should be a lie. Not anything bad, just different than stated. "What is for dinner, Mom?" "Spaghetti." And then put hamburgers on the table. That sort of thing. We could see if Jonathon understands the difference between fact and fiction, truth and untruth. I think we will give it a try. Could be a fun experiment.

Jonathon has been telling people our "good news" quite openly. His story goes something like this: "My mom wrote a note. She said they want to keep me forever. That means it never ends. I will still be with my mom and dad when I am old, like fifteen." It is wonderful to hear him repeat it. We talk about it a lot, trying to make it real. We still do not handle it as earth-shattering excitement, but just as a happy fact. For Jonathon, this seems to be working. He understands, intellectually, what we have done. Emotionally, who knows?

Yesterday Jonathon and I went into Lindsay's class with James. A new girl, Erica, asked me who I was. I told her that I was James' mom, and she was fine with that. Then she asked who Jonathon was. I told her that he was James' brother. She looked at me, looked at Jonathon, looked at James, and then back to me. "But he is black!" I answered that yes, he is black. She then asked; "If he is James' brother, he must be your son. How can he be your son if he is black, and you aren't?" It was such a matter-of-fact question. No negative response, but just innocent curiosity. I told her the basics. "Jonathon had a birth mom who had Jonathon in her tummy. She could not be a good mom for Jonathon, so she decided it was better to find him a home with a mom who could take good care of him. She let me be his mom. Now he is my son." Erica was happy with my answer, and went around reporting the news to a few other children (and, later, to Lindsay.)

Jonathon has started telling us more about some of the abuse he experienced in his last home. It is quite horrible to hear, but I want him to feel free to share it with us. We accept it, and tell him we are sad that those things happened to him. We tell him that little boys and girls should not be treated like that, and that we will make sure that those things do not happen to him again. We do not want to over-indulge him when he shares these things. That could encourage him to make things up to keep being treated special. We also do not want to make too little of it, and make him feel that he is not justified to feel like he was wronged. It is a fine line.

Based on what I am learning from Jonathon's files, I think that Jonathon clearly had attachment issues before he first went into foster care. There is no doubt that his early history was not conducive to bonding. On top of that, it appears that he had one particularly horrible placement, where he was not accepted, and was physically and emotionally abused. Given that past, and the fact that we are attempting to parent him completely differently, could he see enough of a difference here that he is learning to trust us at such an early stage in our lives together? I feel like I am seeing him trust and accept us, but do not want to read too much into it. On the other hand, I do not want to miss important signals that he may be giving us. What is a mom to do?

Jonathon has had very good days since our announcement of his permanent place in our home. It has only been six days, but it has been a great six days! Is this a honeymoon period, with the testing period coming soon? We think it probably is, but will not be heartbroken if we find that we are wrong!

We are enjoying this peaceful phase, and the bonds it is building between all of the children. I am thankful for this time. Even if it does not last long, it is renewing our spirits.

Lori

May 11, 2001

Dear Lori,

As the history rolls out (in frustratingly small bits, over time), it will be important to continue wondering about when the attachment problems began; what exceptions might there ever have been to his life narrative, as that narrative emerged in the first year; who sticks in his mind as a foundation of safety, or a source of affection, or a secure-spot-in-a-storm? When he is 20 and trying to put together a life, and values, and self-control, these things will be critical determinants of his behavior. Even the most minor early, positive experience might make the difference between acting out or controlling himself; loving or hitting; permitting himself the vulnerability of deep connections with another, or engaging only in shallow, serial relationships. It always astonishes me, in my work with adults, the things that make the difference, decades later.

Michael

May 12, 2001

Michael,

I dislike thinking about the things that have happened to my Jonathon, but find myself needing to. I would give anything to be able to go back in time and make things better for him, but I can't. I pray that what I can do from this point forward will be enough for him. He has really been hurt, and we realize this more and more each day. He has started to share things at an accelerated rate in the past week. He began as soon as we announced that he was our son forever.

One of Jonathon's placements was disrupted when the parents decided they just couldn't take it anymore. It was clear, at the relinquishment, that this mom had detached emotionally. Her notes about Jonathon have become profoundly interesting to me, over time. They are typed in all caps, with no punctuation, and many misspellings: "WHEN JONATHON FIRST CAME HE HAD NOT CHOOSEN (sic) A HAND PRFERENCE. HOWEVER SINCE HE HAS BEEN WITH US HE HAS SHOWN A PREFERENCE FOR BEING LEFT HANDED. HE STIL HAS SOME DIFFICULTY HOLDING THINGS LIKE PENCILS AND UTINSILS (sic)." This is the most important stuff she can think of to convey about her foster son? She ends with, "HE FRE-QUENTLY SPEAKS TO STRANGERS, AND WILL GO UP AND TALK TO JUST ABOUT ANYONE." That was her note. Her partner left a hand-written note, talking about Jonathon's "...total invasion of personal space", while complaining of his jealousy of another child in the home. She ends with, "Struck family dog without provocation. Furiously stomps on insects. Obsessed with guns and knives. Very frequent lies. Pretending ignorance of information we feel he knows. Increase in mas-turbation at inappropriate places." Everything in that note was negative.

After Jonathon came into our home, he mentioned hitting, and cringed anytime anyone moved a hand quickly. Jon noticed this in therapy, and we noticed it at home. The other things that we noted early on were: Jonathon panicked anytime he saw a car that reminded him of the one at the previ-ous foster home. He swore he saw the foster mom drive by one day when we were out shopping, and another time when we were on our way to ther-apy. Both times he cried and asked me to keep her away. He asked me, many times, if she knew where we lived. Jonathon mentioned lots of stand-ing up for long time-outs, but we never thought too much of that. What is "long", to a child? Going through Jonathon's photos, there are several of him in time-out. One photo shows Jonathon, wearing a snowsuit, crying. He is covered in snow. He says that he was freezing cold, and that the foster mom made him sit outside for "a long time".

In the past week, Jonathon has made a few new comments. This has all happened since we told him that he was going to stay here forever. One day he was using the bathroom, and missed the toilet a little bit. He told me about it, and then said, "My other foster mom made me lick it up." I asked him what he was talking about, and he said, "When I missed at [my other home], she made me lick it up. She said she was tired of me missing." I asked him to show me what he was talking about by pointing and telling me what happened. He took me into the bathroom, and pointed to the opened back of the toilet seat. He said, "I missed, and my pee got there. She told me to clean it up. I started to, and she said, 'No, lick it up' so I had to lick it up." I asked him what he did when she told him to lick it up. He said, "I cried, and told her that was a bad thing to do. She made me do it anyway."

Yesterday, Jonathon asked me if it was okay to hold people's heads under water so they couldn't breathe. I responded, "Do you mean like in the swimming pool? That is how you can learn to hold your breath, if you put your head under water for just a little time." He said; "No, Mom. I mean like in the bathtub. Like when my other mom was mad at me and held my head under water because she was mad and wanted me to be good."

This is what I know: I know that I am sick at the thought of these things happening to my little boy. I believe his stories, and am furious that this kind of abuse occurred. What else will he share, I wonder? I hope there is not more. I am sure there probably is. I will not prompt him, but will listen as he decides to share. I want him to feel safe, secure in opening up, and I want to assure him that those things were wrong and will not happen to him again.

I am worried about the involvement of Child Protective Services, and wonder if they will want to talk to Jonathon. If so, I need to find out what our rights are. I will not allow anyone to talk to him alone, and really do not want him to talk to anybody new. My desire is to protect him, but I know there is a concern for the child still in the home. Suggestions?

Those are the things I know at this point. That is the first time I have stated them all together. I just read back over what I have written, and I feel numb. And I am crying. What on earth does my sweet child feel as he shares all of this? How can anyone hurt a child? How can I help my child, who has been so badly hurt?

I need to share some good things, now. Siobhan was here Thursday morning, when Jonathon woke up. We heard a sweet little voice at the top of the stairs. "Mommy?" I looked up at him, and he came down the stairs and into my arms. He just snuggled against me, with his head on my shoulder. I gave him a kiss, and said; "Good morning, sweet boy. Did you have a good sleep? Mommy loves you." He kissed my neck, said he loved me, too, and kept snuggling. For the next five minutes, as Siobhan and I continued to talk, Jonathon snuggled. He would lay his head on my shoulder, and then lift his head and gaze at my face. I would gaze into his eyes, give him a kiss, and he would lay his head back down. This has become our routine in the mornings, although usually not standing at the front door. For the last two weeks or so, I have seen this time become longer and more intimate. A real time of connection. That morning, as Siobhan left us and drove to work, she says that she cried all the way there. She realized she had witnessed a precious, wonderful moment that is typical for very young children and their mommies.

You cannot possibly know how much the Thomas family appreciates you! Between you and Jon, you have made this adoption possible.

Lori

May 12, 2001

Dear Lori,

My stepson, Jeremy is lying on the floor of my office, rather absent-mindedly playing with some of the infant toys I have in here, while I think about the historical material you sent about Jonathon and prepare to write to you. Jeremy has been very touchy the past couple of weeks, really struggling with some memories of violence, and some aggressive feelings inside. But I think there might be more: it's Mother's Day tomorrow. I think the meaning of that day, for many adoptees, is often invisible (even to the child) but rarely innocuous.

So I brought it up tonight, at dinner. Jeremy said he didn't know what he was feeling, but he made no effort to deny that his insides were in a stew. I brought up the "wig hat" (you will remember that story, I am sure), and wondered if we needed to get it out and see what it might have to say, and he jumped at the idea. He even added the details: we would need to go to the exercise room in the basement, I would need to get on the treadmill, and THEN he could ask the wig hat about his feelings.

So we did. But—as is so often the case with ANY kids, much less ones with so much hurt—it must have been a little too late in the evening, or he was a little too scared, or SOMETHING. I pumped away, trying to appear just interested enough, but not TOO interested. He had trouble finding the wig hat. He kept wondering if I was too tired. After a while, we wandered to the next room (my office), where he presented me with a certificate of recognition (a fake $5 bill from one of his games), and then he lay down on the carpet and began playing with the baby toys. I started to read your messages from this morning. He told me he liked me, but that he liked his real dad more. I said that of course he did. He was his real dad, and I wasn't. He asked, "What makes him my real dad?" Then, "no, never mind about that".

I am acutely aware that it is almost Mother's Day. While he claims he can't think how he would like to honor his first mother, his birth mother, and pretends that he is not thinking of her, I DO wonder what part is being played, in his extreme edginess the past couple of weeks, by the approach of the day that is, after all, about his FIRST LOSS.

Life with ALL children is SO strange, isn't it? Why are we in their lives? Why are they in OURS?

Your agitation about the misspellings in the former foster mother's notes was funny. What'sa matter? Just couldn't come out and say what you really WANTED to say? "THEY WERE IDIOTS! THEY DON'T EVEN KNOW THIS CHILD WHO COMMUNICATES SO CLEARLY—EVEN IF IT IS UPSIDE-DOWN—WHAT HE NEEDS. THEY HURT MY SON, DAMNIT! AND THEY CAN'T EVEN SPELL!!!"

The differences between you (your family) and them are revealed in just the one line in your message: your incredulous rhetorical question about how they could think, as they had learned that they could not handle Jonathon with just one additional human child in the mix, that he would be better off in a large group [daycare]. A painful discovery of my own, that must be re-discovered weekly, and never stops shocking and hurting, is that a good deal of the world is utterly cut off from remembering (yes, it is partly that: it's not just head knowledge, it's remembering) what little children feel and what they need and how the world looks to them. To you it was obvious, but you were making the fatal error of thinking about it as a child would. This puts you in a different world. To you, things seem clear. Casework decisions, parenting choices, judicial decisions—all of these are in sharp, principled focus for you, because you seem, for some reason, to REMEMBER. And so it is bizarre and dreadful, to you, when people don't and, as a result, make the stupidest choices, or the most narcissistic choices, or the choices that so clearly avoid the pleas of the child to consider the obvious, to consider his heart.

No, I don't have suggestions about possible CPS involvement that will make it all right for Jonathon. I know you don't need me to tell you:

A. They are not likely, at the time of any investigation regarding the safety of another child, to have overriding concern for the safety of the child from whom they wish to get information (Jonathon). At that moment, in my experience, they are thinking of one child and one child only, and tend to have blinders on for the possibility that their own efforts to protect that child may abuse another.

B. There is the risk that the inquiry will be carried out by someone who knows almost nothing about children, even less about Jonathon, and is not even particularly skilled at interviewing.

C. You may be cast as intrusive, over-protective, even uncaring about the little girl remaining in the other foster home (if you look out for Jonathon's interests).

D. It will be hard to tell exactly what your rights are (tho' it might help to ask someone there who knows) because the authorities will be so driven to do what they need to do (and are required to do) that they may act as if you have no rights at all (and Jonathon even fewer).

E. It is fairly likely that an investigation will be traumatic for Jonathon.

F. The tanks that you are thinking about lining up around your front door will probably not amuse the authorities (which is not to say that you shouldn't get on with the business of lining them up!).

G. Anybody that messes with Jonathon Thomas is likely to regret it, (if they live that long), 'lessen I miss my guess…

Michael

May 13, 2001

Michael,

My Mother's Day thoughts:

I have just finished reading *Everyday Blessings*, by Myla and Jon Kabat-Zinn. I loved reading the book, and was intrigued by the concepts. I find the parenting styles similar to my own, but the foundation of my family is quite different than theirs. I parent with a very strong Christian ethic and belief, while the Kabat-Zinn family espouses the mindfulness based on Buddhist beliefs.

Why do I parent the way I do? On this day, Mother's Day, I find it something to contemplate.

I do have a solid inner life, including meditation. A favorite verse is in Jeremiah: "For I know the plans I have for you, says the Lord. They are plans for good and not for evil, plans to give you a hope and a future."

What do I believe about children? First, I know beyond the shadow of a doubt that children—all of them—are a blessing. Christ, contrary to the customs of the times, took time to listen and pay attention to children. The humility, wonder, and faith of children are hard to match. When we try, we truly find joy in the small details of life. In *Everyday Blessings* the authors talk about experiencing the here and now, and remind us not to lose THIS moment while fretting about another. I find, in my life, that it is the little moments, and our reaction to them, that affect my children most deeply. It is not the sermons and big lessons, but the everyday living that makes them who they are. What an opportunity we have as parents! As Thoreau said, in *Walden Pond*, "To affect the quality of the day, that is the highest of arts."

What are we to do with the difficult moments? How we see things affects our response. Is the child being curious or disobedient? Can we find humor and joy, rather than irritation and dismay? I find that this is similar to the concept of "The Attitude" in *Building the Bonds of Attachment*, by Daniel Hughes. A positive attitude about children, and about life, sure goes a long way toward enjoying it all.

In *Everyday Blessings*, the sovereignty of the child is stressed. I find this to be a concept clearly depicted in the story of the prodigal son. What did the prodigal's parents do? When the child rebelled, they accepted his choices. They let him go, make his mistakes, and reap the consequences. I am sure they counseled him and asked him to reconsider, but then accepted his decision. Getting himself into an awful situation got his attention, and caused him to change. The prodigal son came to his senses, and re-evaluated his life. While this was going on, his parents were in the background, praying and waiting. How did they respond when the son returned? With a lecture, and "I told you so"? No, they loved him back into the family. They treated him, smelly and all, as royalty. They loved him, accepted him, and forgave him completely. What a wonderful example of parenting through a tough time!

Okay, so you hit the nail on the head about my misspelling comment. THEY WERE IDIOTS! Jon has been teaching Jonathon to get in touch with his feelings, and be able to identify them. I guess I am learning, too. So here goes: (I am yelling) I AM MAD, MICHAEL! HOW COULD THEY HURT MY LITTLE BOY LIKE THAT? I AM VERY, REALLY MAD! (Jonathon has a habit of saying "very, really".) I feel a little better now. Not much, but a little.

I am very concerned about the possible CPS involvement, but do not plan to sit by quietly and allow anyone to interview my son. I will do what I can, and plan to stay on my toes. I am hoping any information they need from Jonathon can be gathered through non-intrusive methods, like sitting in on therapy without interfering. I will talk to Jon, and see where we go from here.

Lori

May 16, 2001

Michael,

I flew up to Barrie last night to help my eldest son, Joshua, move back down to Virginia.

When we discussed my trip with Jonathon during therapy on Monday, he cried real tears—sad ("I am going to miss my mommy") tears! He hugged me, and told me how much he would miss me. I assured him that I would be returning in three days, and that I would miss him, too. (In fact, I miss him terribly. Leaving my children has never been top on my list, but leaving one like Jonathon, at such a vulnerable time in his life, was almost impossible.)

Jonathon cries easily. There is the, "I didn't get my way" cry, and the, "I think they will get me this toy if I look REALLY sad" cry. There is a lot of frustration-crying. Most of his crying has looked a lot like manipulation. Not much crying when he hurts himself. Anger is more common at those times. And I have not seen much sad crying. Most of the sad crying that we have seen has been in therapy.

So there we are, in therapy, with Jonathon crying because he will miss his mommy! Jon let us both know how very good it is to be able to miss someone. Jonathon does not seem to worry that I will return, which is another great sign. Before I left yesterday, Jonathon hugged me and told me that he would see me when I come back on Friday.

Back in January and February, when Jonathon was still a very new member of the Thomas home, Jonathon would react strongly each time someone returned home from a trip to the store (or anyplace, for that matter). He would run to the door, yelling, "I KNEW you would come back!" Of course, we took that to mean that he did NOT know if we would come back or not, regardless of how much we assured him that we would be returning. Now, a few months later, the greeting is more along the lines of "Mommy, I missed you." Then he gives a hug, and off to play he goes. Seeing this progress in our new son thrills us to our very core.

Paul has taken the next few days off, so that he can be home with the children while I am away. They will probably all sleep until noon and then eat junk for breakfast! I am sure they will have a great daddy-time.

Lori

May 19, 2001

Dear Lori,

I can only begin to imagine your pleasure at the particular brand of tears you saw this week, about your departure. It did wonders for me to hear that Paul stayed home with the kids during your absence. I hope they did, indeed, do some crazy, can't-get-away-with-this-when-Mom-is-here stuff. I wonder when Jonathon needed to act out about your being away: with Paul, not until your return, or still holding together until he can't, anymore? (Do I make it sound as if it's inevitable? Seems likely to me that it is.)

Michael

May 19, 2001

Michael,

Do you happen to have some kind of "bugging device" in our home? You ALWAYS seem to know exactly what is happening! I left on Tuesday, and Jonathon decided to start defying Paul pretty constantly on Wednesday. Nothing horrible, just the complete defiance that we came to know so very well a few months ago. Today, my first day back, Jonathon had to have some pretty intense holding times, and fought against being held by Paul or making any eye contact with him. As I write this, Jonathon has been in bed for two hours, "trying" to get to sleep. I was in there a few minutes ago, rubbing his back and calming him down. As he settled, he talked to me through his stuffed seal. He has named the seal "Gidget", like our dog. He calls her "Giggie", like we call him "Johnny". He talked to the seal, and asked her questions about himself. "Giggie, why was Jonathon screaming in the bathtub when Daddy told him it was time to get out?" Giggie would then give the answers to me. (Giggie explained to me, very patiently, that Jonathon thought he should play in the bathtub a little bit longer while James got dressed.) It has been interesting to watch Jonathon go through this process of missing me, acting out, and then allowing me back into his home and heart after three days away.

While my son, Joshua and I spent 16 hours in the car yesterday, we got into a serious discussion about Winnie-the-Pooh and his friends. I have decided that Christopher Robin has a good way of presenting "The Attitude". He sees Pooh mess up, time after time. Pooh just plain and simple has no common sense, and he is very impulsive. Both are characteristics that I see in Jonathon. Christopher Robin never yells or becomes frustrated with Pooh. He just sighs, calls Pooh a "silly old bear", and loves him, unconditionally. Christopher Robin tries to help Pooh with some problem-solving, but mostly I see him as a supportive and loving friend.

It is great to be home, and to have my whole family together for a time.

Lori

May 20, 2001

Dear Lori,

Funny, I'd never thought much about the matter of Pooh. Sure clicks.

No, no bugging device. Paul must have felt as if he had been hit with a sledge hammer: the BIG DECISION just made, you were gone for the first time, and here he is with World War III in his lap and no big answers (just BIG QUESTIONS!). Do you happen to remember the little girl I mentioned (by way of example) in the "Multiple Transitions" film? She really DID take a dump in front of her foster parents' bedroom door every night for three weeks, following their departure for a short trip. She said nary a word, gave not the slightest indication that she would miss them before they left, that she was missing them while they were gone, or that she had missed them, when they returned. Indeed, she barely acknowledged they had come back. She just got up in the night and left part of herself near where they were sleeping. I don't think they made the connection, and she sure didn't help make it clear to them.

Amazing to hear that you had a "wig hat" sort of experience! Sure makes sense, doesn't it, that talking through "Giggie" feels ever so much easier than using his own mouth?

Michael

May 20, 2001

Michael,

I have just tucked the boys into bed, and tried to settle them down, and feel like this might be another LONG night! Before going to bed, Jonathon used the bathroom. I reminded him to be careful with his aim, as this is often a difficulty for him. When he came out of the bathroom, he announced that he had aimed very carefully. A few minutes later, when I went in to use the bathroom myself, I found that he had, indeed, aimed very carefully. There is no way in the world to get that much urine on a toilet seat unless you really give it your best shot! I do not plan to mention it to Jonathon tonight, but will wait until he goes to use the bathroom again tomorrow. I think I will bring it up in a funny kind of way, and see how he responds. (Yes, I do remember about the little girl in the video who expressed herself so very clearly in front of her parents' bedroom door.)

Jonathon clearly is letting me know that leaving him was a very, really bad idea. He did not appreciate it, and has reverted to being a completely disobedient, very bouncy kind of boy. The good news is that Paul and I anticipated this kind of regression, and are not too worried about it. We are not enjoying it, but we are not in a panic. It is kind of funny, really. Jonathon's unpredictability is so predictable that you knew it was happening from many miles away. So we are back in a "holding pattern" of sorts. Lots of it! Literally.

I read *Winnie the Pooh and Tigger Too* tonight. Tigger is bouncing along, frustrating many of his friends. The words, "By the time Tigger bounced away, Rabbit's whole garden was ruined" really hit me. The physical destruction possible when a RAD child comes into the home is pretty incredible, isn't it? I need to re-frame at least three pictures. Seems the glass in them breaks if something hard is thrown at them. The furniture does not stand much of a chance. I have decided to put off buying a china cabinet for a bit longer. Carpet will need to be replaced in a couple of areas (permanent marker). The car, the toys, the house... They are all just "things", and a small price to pay in the bigger scheme of things. We are working on a life here, and building character in a lot of other lives. We will care for our "stuff" to the best of our ability, but we will not fret overly much if some of the "stuff" does not survive the storms that keep sweeping through our home.

Paul and I do not have any doubt that we made the right decision about adoption. These little setbacks just let us see how damaged Jonathon was, and how important it is for him to have some stability in order to heal. Life sure has some funny twists! We will do our best to enjoy them.

Lori

May 25, 2001

Michael,

We had a horrendous post-placement visit with our social worker yesterday. Jonathon showed her his "best" attachment-disorder side. I had already shared with her how he had had a rough week since I went away last week, so I hope she expected some bad. She got it! Nothing in particular, just defiance and rudeness and a few bad words ("stupid", "shut-up", "butt"). He did his best to get me rattled, and to show her what he is capable of. We had some holding time, and some screaming by Jonathon, and he squirted us with a hose, at one point. I would love to see how she writes the report! I am not concerned. I was not surprised, and she should not have been, either. I don't think it alarmed her, but I know that we both would have been happier if the visit had taken place during a better time in Jonathon's adjustment. Maybe next visit...

Lori

May 30, 2001

Dear Michael,

Hope you do not mind me writing again, so soon. I just need to share some thoughts, to keep myself sane.

Jonathon's behavior and moods are all over the place. I have seen some wild shifts in the past 24 hours.

Jonathon woke up in the middle of the night and climbed into our bed. This is unusual for him. He told me that he was having scary thoughts, and wanted to be with me. He cuddled, but could not fall back asleep. The more I tried to soothe him, the more wiggly he became. So I stopped soothing, and was just there, for him. He settled down a bit, but never went back to sleep. By morning, he was quite the wild child: bad words, inappropriate laughing, jumping, wiggling, incessant chatter... We held and talked, and it seemed to have no impact. Then Jonathon decided he would like to watch a cartoon. I usually am not too excited about that, in the mornings. This morning, I was all too happy to turn on a show and see if Jonathon could settle down and watch it. He did. He actually sat still for 30 minutes. After the show, it was time for break-fast. I announced that I was going into the kitchen to get breakfast, and Jonathon ran off into another room. He was being defiant, and told me he was not going to eat. I continued to get things ready, and just ignored Jonathon's comments. Suddenly, he was at the piano. He "plays" piano once in a while, and his playing usually reflects his mood. As Jonathon started to play, I expected wild, banging noises. Instead, I heard him play-ing gently. It was soft, peaceful playing. After 20 minutes, he came into the kitchen. "Did you like my music, Mom?" I told him I loved it, and thought it was beautiful. He then went to the table to eat his breakfast.

Jonathon became rather animated again, after breakfast, and started running around like a wild man. I feel like he is on the verge of explod-ing, and it is a constant struggle to keep him together. I do not know if I am doing the right thing by trying to avoid the explosion. Maybe he needs to explode, and get it over with. I don't know. Just thinking.

Thankfully, we have therapy today. It could not come at a better time!
Lori

May 30, 2001

Dear Lori,

I presume your wonderful therapist gives you ideas about what to do at home—or, more correctly put, what to TRY at home. These cycles you describe are both unusual/unpredictable and typical. Jonathon always seems to surprise, tho', doesn't he? I guess the only thing that is clear is what an amazing turmoil flies about inside of him. You seem to have plenty of perspective about that. It seems to help when it can be communicated to the child—sometimes in words, sometimes only in attitude—that you know he is as troubled as you are by his behavior, and that you know he wants to manage it better. In other words, it seems to be meaningful to frame things such that it is YOU AND JONATHON (united) AGAINST THE MAD, rather than YOU AGAINST JONATHON, or YOU AGAINST JONATHON'S BEHAVIOR.

Jeremy is not quite as volatile, these days, but is certainly surprising and unpredictable. Sometimes "squishing" helps enormously (in which Mary rolls him up in a blanket and lies gently on top of him), and he has been especially asking for that these past few days. Other days, he doesn't want to be touched, recoils from touch. Some days he just can't stop pounding his chest; on other days, he walks around singing like an angel. One day he was gentle and quiet when he came home from school. However, Mary was not yet back from an errand, and I was down in my office, with a patient. He positioned himself on the couch, directly above my office, and began to pound the coffee table with his foot, until I had to interrupt the session and go upstairs and ask him to please stop. (I know: we are blessed that we can even THINK about his managing himself without adult supervision immediately available. I got my attitude there, after fuming about having to interrupt a therapy session!)

The thing that uplifts me greatly is your ability to hold on to the notion that Jonathon's behavior MAKES SENSE, even tho' it may not seem to, at the moment, or the exact interpretation isn't immediately available. The behavior is STILL annoying or hurtful or fretful, but it sure makes a difference in MY heart, anyway, when I can rest assured that the behavior is meaningful, rather than random. Clinically, I also happen to know it's true—not just an artifact that I create to feel more comfortable.

The thing that breaks my heart (not entirely in a soft or empathic way—there is some anger and fear in me about it) is the HUGE QUESTION about what sort of heart Jeremy has. We watched "The Color Purple" together (as a family) the other night. As usual, he laughed when other people were hurting, tapped his feet incessantly, showed not the slightest sign of feeling when the movie was intensely sad (and everyone else in the room was crying), and even had to ask his mother why she had tears on her face. He wasn't being mean, but his obliviousness gets me, sometimes. Character and heart were such important parts of my growing up—thanks largely to my grandparents, rather than my parents—and I can hardly stand the thought that there is such emptiness in him. Mary counters that he seems to get upset, sometimes, when she is crying or otherwise upset, and she thinks this is a sign of empathy. I think it is not; instead, I think it is simply fear/anxiety about whether HE will be safe, at the moment, if his mother is troubled. Pure (and perfectly understandable) narcissism. Nothing malicious about it, I know, but pure narcissism rattles me. Maybe there is more in there: a softness that will come out, someday.

I could certainly "hear" the fretting in your email "voice". This is hard work, isn't it?

Michael

May 30, 2001

Michael,

Remember our thoughts on Winnie-the-Pooh and the possible examples of good therapeutic processes contained in Pooh's stories? I was rather amazed the other night, as I looked for the next book to read on the shelves of Barnes and Noble, that books have been written about Pooh and friends. I am about to begin *Pooh and the Psychologists,* by Jon Tyerman Williams, which presents POOH as the brilliant psychotherapist, and uses the example of Eeyore as a case of clinical depression.

Another book that I just picked up is *Becoming Attached* by Robert Karen. As I read this, I am becoming more interested in reading some of Bowlby's work. This whole field of attachment work is so intriguing to me. I just wish that I had done some of this reading BEFORE I had the opportunity to parent my dear Jonathon.

I really appreciate your reminder about framing things as US AND JONATHON against the mad, or the bad… That is an important distinction, and I do not know how well we have done with that. I really want Jonathon to know that we are with him, on the same side of this war that we seem to be fighting. He needs allies and advocates. That is our role. Help us to remember that when we grow weary.

Today I received a message from the social worker from our local CPS who will interview Jonathon as they continue to investigate past abuse. I called a social worker that I know and trust, and asked her opinion about the CPS worker. She knows him and his work, and says that we will be in good hands. I sure do hope she is right. I will be very relieved when the investigation is complete. In the meantime, I plan to be very cautious about what I agree to. I do not want Jonathon hurt in any way, and I cannot imagine that this process will be without some pain.

How can anybody hurt a child? I know how easy it is to get frustrated, and even angry, but how can someone actually reach out and hurt a precious little boy? Just thinking about it makes me want to vomit.

You mentioned in one of your last emails that parenting these special children (or maybe it is children in general) is really hard work. I could not agree more. There are days when it is so frustrating, and seems so hopeless, that I wonder why we are working so hard at it. And then there are days that are so joyful and fulfilling that I wonder why I thought it was such hard work just the other day. And then another tough day comes. Or many of them in a row. Breakthroughs, followed by regression, followed by a moment of bliss. Huge hope, and then hopelessness, and then back to huge hope again. If this work were based on feelings, and rewards, then no one would be foolish enough to continue. But we base our work on KNOWING that it is the right thing to do. It is the only hope these kids have of making it. There is no guarantee that we will be successful, and I know that. But there is a guarantee that if a child like Jonathon is left in a life of instability, he will NOT make it. Any hope is better than none. Every child deserves a chance. In our case, we are incredibly fortunate. We have taken Jonathon in at a young age, and he seems not nearly as broken as some children that I have read about. He is a great boy, with lots of love and sweetness to share. He wants to love, and to be loved. He is receptive to therapy, and wants to heal. These are not conscious thoughts on Jonathon's part, of course, but as we work with him we see great potential. We really have lots of reasons for lots of hope. I do not know how I would cope if we went long periods of time with no progress. That would be truly tough.

I just got a phone call. Another home-schooling mom called to let me know that a mutual friend lost her husband tonight. This dad of eight was out for an evening run, and when he came home he had a heart attack. Their eight children range from kindergarten to high school, and they are an incredibly sweet family. I cannot imagine their pain. We will pull together as a group, and do anything we can for them. We are all stunned.

Suddenly, the issues that my family faces seem rather minor.

I'll write again soon. I sure do appreciate these conversations.

Lori

May 31, 2001

Lori,

I started wondering if your oft-stated question "How can anyone hurt a child?" might, actually, be non-rhetorical. Your reading choices make it seem that something about this is brewing in you. I think I'll send a copy of a recent short paper of mine that addresses the very question, by way of a case study.

A wet day here in the woods, as I sit awaiting my next patient: a mom who was divorced from her 11-year-old son's dad a few years back, raged at him for the next few years, remarried, then separated from that fellow last fall. She is here to discover the "mystery" about why her son is withdrawn, disobedient and disrespectful. Not too much mystery, I'm guessing...

Michael

May 31, 2001

Michael,

I have a theory about your patient. You know: the mom who divorced, raged, remarried, divorced? The child's withdrawal, disrespect, etc. is clearly due to his diet. Could not possibly be anything else. Pooh would probably recommend a smakerel of honey to cure what ails the young man.

I joke about how many children we have, and how they got here, and Paul always plays the, "How did you talk me into this?" role. The truth, of course, is that he would have it no other way. He stands as my voice of reason, and sometimes holds off on decisions longer than I would like. He is my balance. Otherwise, I might not think things through fully, before jumping into a situation. My heart guides me, where his brain guides him. It has actually worked out rather well. He is a terrific father, and lets the kids know that he cherishes them. He is a rare find. I am glad I found him, as there could not be many men out there who would put up with me. (On Monday, we celebrated 21 years together.)

Jonathon is starting to calm down again, and some of the regression (aggression, disobedience, bouncing off the walls) that we have been experiencing since my trip to Canada has begun to diminish. We are focusing much of his energy into baseball and wrestling. I hear Jonathon downstairs right now, doing jumping jacks with Rebecca. It sounds like he did twenty, and seems pretty happy with that.

Jonathon is easily distracted, and has a very hard time going to bed at night. We cannot leave James and Jonathon in the same bedroom. When we take James out to go to sleep with Rebecca, or in our room, Jonathon settles down much easier. James just wants to sleep at night, but Jonathon would much rather say bad words and get James to giggle. Then the circus begins. They feed off each other's energy, and soon the whole house is roaring with life again. It is not good for James, or for Jonathon.

Morning time has become very cuddly with Jonathon. He wakes up and seeks me out immediately. He likes to be held, and allows me to rub his head, kiss his cheek, hug him, and rock him. He hugs back, and is pretty affectionate while he is still sleepy. I take full advantage of that time, and do nothing but hold Jonathon. I am feeling very good about our morning ritual, and the bonding that seems to occur. It is the only time that such a level of affection is happily tolerated by Jonathon.

I just received a phone call from the CPS worker, who needs to interview Jonathon. He is insistent upon talking to Jonathon alone, and I am not sure how I feel about that. I want to at least be a presence, and a place of safety and retreat for my son. I asked the worker to call Jon (our therapist) and talk to him. I need to think about what I really think is best, here. How hard do I want to fight, and which fights do I want to choose? My choice would be to just go off to the mountains with my boy, and have a nice, quiet life. I would take the whole family, of course. Grow our own vegetables, and tell the world to get lost. Then no one could hurt my boy, again! The only problem with that scenario is that we do not want to live a nice, quiet life in the mountains. We like being an active part of a community. Other than that, we would be out of here!

I will anticipate reading the "How can anyone hurt a child?" paper. I am struggling with forgiving those who hurt Jonathon, in the past. I need to forgive, and do not want to harbor any bitterness. That does not help me or my son. I want to do what is best and right, but I also want to scream! Can I both forgive *and* scream?

Lori

May 31, 2001

Dear Lori,

My God, what was I thinking? Of course: DIET!!! Why did you wait until they left; I could have instructed them to just feed him fewer tomatoes and smaller servings (at least) of sweet potatoes (NO BUTTER) and obedience would return. Sometimes I am SO dense.

Think about a transitional object for Jonathon, during the CPS interview. I was pretty sure they would demand to talk with him alone, but you can have a presence by way of an object that the two of you choose (or you can just let him) that will represent the solidity and safety of you, or Paul or your family. He can have it with him throughout; depending on his experience with such things, you may need to help him know how to use it ("Stick it in your pocket, and you can touch it if you get a little worried, or if you're not sure what to say; hug it tighter if the questions seem confusing, and it will help the fog go away, so you will know just what to do or say").

Something I learned many years ago—when studying parents who had a child with a serious physical disability—amazed me (since so much is written about UNITY in marriage, and so little about DIFFERENT-NESS and BALANCE): how well a family can operate when parents assume roles quite different from one another. What a wonderful thing for kids, too (again, contrary to what is often written): they get TWO versions of how to act, TWO models for how to be, and they get to see two respectable (and respectful) people holding on to themSELVES, while cooperating with another.

Michael

May 31, 2001

Michael,

Give me 24 hours' notice, and I will be happy to share my theories on the rest of your patients, too. Then you will be free to perfect your game of golf. Or take up golf, if it is not already on your schedule.

Now, if only I could come up with some good ideas to cure the children in my own home!

We just returned from Patrick's baseball game. James, after some unsuccessful attempts to play with the other children, chose to befriend a woman with a blanket. He shared with her all of his airplane knowledge. "Pilot sit cockpit. Where airplane go? I go Mickey Mouse. Who baby-sit airplane? Airplane fly over house." I think she was duly impressed.

I know you are right about using a transitional object for Jonathon during the CPS interview. That is a perfect idea! The current plan is to do the interview here, at home, so he will be comfortable with the setting. Jonathon has a stuffed seal that he loves, and we often cuddle with it together. I think Seal needs to be at the interview. I have a necklace that Jonathon loves. It is a shiny pineapple, and he asks to wear it often. Maybe he would like to wear it, during the interview. He loves the way it feels and shines. I have let him wear it before, when he was concerned about my leaving. It seems to give him the needed assurance that I will return. I will coach him on the use of seal and/or pineapple, and maybe we will get through this just fine.

I think I am just beginning to know Jonathon. I look into his eyes, and am finding a person there. As a mom taking in a hurt child, it is easy to see the brokenness, the hurt, and the need. Paul gave me an analogy to help me sort out my thoughts on Jonathon. Jonathon is like a young tree, damaged by pests and storms. The trunk survived, and is still a very good little tree. Some of the branches are damaged, however, and need to be pruned in order to avoid robbing the tree of much-needed energy to continue to grow. That pruning, in Jonathon's life, is our effort to help him heal from the bad and sad parts of his early years. Our goal there is to work until we have a healthy trunk, as free from the damage as possible. That is the first work to be done with Jonathon. The second work, (and the works will necessarily overlap) is the building work. With the tree, that would be making sure it gets the fertilizer and water and sunlight and whatever else it needs to grow big and healthy. This young tree that we start with is not the final goal, it is just the first phase in the overall life of the tree. This second work is the molding, character-building part of Jonathon's life. This is what equips him to be a moral, upright, solid young person in the future. Does this make sense?

So now that we have our tree analogy, all I can picture is Pooh Bear hovering over the tree with a big, black rain cloud balloon. Guess I had better do some reading on *Pooh and the Psychologists.*

Lori

June 2, 2001

Michael,

Wow! Thanks for sending me your paper ("Reconstructing the Parent's Infant Narrative: An Approach to Child Abuse Treatment"). The parent's infant narrative is clearly key to his/her behavior as a parent, and the paper answered so many questions for me. It helps me tremendously, in regard to understanding and, hopefully, forgiving those who have abused my little Jonathon in his past.

Given the understanding, and the forgiving, many questions remain in my mind. Actually, they are new questions, brought forward as I read your paper.

What are we to do when a parent is not open to exploring themselves? Clearly, you were able to help Kathrynn (in the paper's case study) explore her past without her even really realizing what she was doing. That was possible because you had a reason, professionally, to be there, providing access that was so vital to her road to recovery. What happens when the help is not accepted? Or, more likely, when the help that is offered is not the right help? Let's face it. There are not enough MICHAELs out there. Too many times these parents are going to be faced with a slap on the wrist, and a parenting class. What will happen to their children?

I know *of* the abuser, but do not know her. I hate her for the abuse she inflicted upon my son, but do not want to hate. I can forgive her, but can I help her? In the meantime, my primary role, as I see it, is to help the child that was abused. Clearly, he is now my job. I know that her abuse, inflicted upon him, is only a part of what has hurt him so deeply. There are many other parts to his past, with which he must now deal, and from which he must heal. That is the job that I KNOW I have. Is there any point in him ever having contact with any of his abusers again? (Not next week or month. But is there a need sometime out there? Or is he best served by my acknowledging his hurt, his being protected from future abuse, and his never needing to see his abuser again?)

The question of abuse remains. Why DOES a parent abuse a child? It is an emotionally disturbing point to ponder. Are there those who were parented well, but just plain choose evil over good? For whatever reason, they just do not respond to good parenting, and decide to harm others? If the answer does not lie in the parent's infant narrative but, instead, in their childhood or adult lives, can they be reached and helped, with the same success? Does it depend on what trauma might have triggered them?

I am big into scrapbooking with my children. It is so important, and I love including the past with the children who were not in our home from the beginning. I include their past, so that they can share it with us. And I share our past, so that they can feel part of it all. Everyone has their own book, and we have a family album.

A quick Jonathon note that I must share. Yesterday, I was leaving home to run some errands. Jonathon was staying with his siblings, and was fine with that. He gave me a big hug, and told me to drive carefully. Then he looked right into my eyes, and said, "I love you, Mom. Be very careful. Please drive slowly. If you see a kitty, or a squirrel, stop the car. Don't hit them. It would kill them. Be very careful." It seemed such a heavy thought for such a young child. He was worried about me, and the kitties and the squirrels. As far as I know, he has not witnessed an animal being hit by a car. He has certainly seen plenty of road kill here, though.

Squirrels, chipmunks, rabbits, deer; they are all very abundant here and, therefore, we have seen too many of them dead on the roads. Something about the whole dialogue with Jonathon touched me deeply. I don't know if it was the sweetness with which Jonathon expressed himself, or the level of concern he showed. But I was touched.

Lori

June 4, 2001

Dear Lori,

You are quite right about the "slap on the wrist" approach—tho' I see it less as being insufficiently punitive than as being hopelessly naive about what it takes to bring about change. Parents who merely represent the latest generation in a long line of parents in their family history who have abused, or who have been unable to attach to boys, or who molested their girls, or who seem to love pregnancy but hate the actual babies, etc., etc., are ordered to PARENTING CLASSES by the judge or the child welfare worker. The narrative of the parent—the guiding, driving force behind their behavior—will never be touched in a parenting class. Therefore, there will not be change. We will then blame the parent for not trying hard enough, when it is the treatment to which we ordered them that is ill-suited to cure the disease.

There is no answer, of course, to your question about how people can be touched, absent the sort of contracted opportunity I had with Kathryn. I do believe—and this is a combination of my own personal faith, and a particular psychological perspective taught me by my teacher (Selma Fraiberg)—that there is a grinding, powerful force inside of parents that makes them want desperately to make it better for their babies than it was for themselves (when they were babies). Even abusive behavior—often carried out in my presence, with the video camera going— may represent this very struggle; after all, how clever one could say it is for a parent in heaps of trouble (but denying it) to lash out at baby in front of a person like me (or the family doctor, or the nurse at the WIC clinic), an act that just might bring help.

I also believe that God set things up such that babies challenge our very souls. In this way, unhappily, many babies get beaten or ignored or emotionally tortured. At the same time, many babies provoke the healing of old wounds in their mothers and fathers. This is one of the ways, in my view, that we get a little better, each generation.

Michael

June 7, 2001

Michael,

Tuesday morning, about an hour before the CPS interview was to begin, the worker (Frank) called me back. He casually stated that he was returning my call, and wondered what was up. By now, I was tense in anticipation. But I took a deep breath, and repeated my request (for the umpteenth time) that I be allowed to be present as a quiet, calming force for my son. I expected my request to be denied again, and I was prepared to calmly ask to talk to Frank's supervisor. Instead, Frank's very anticlimactic response was, "OK, that will be fine." So the balloon of tension was popped, and Frank said that he would be at our home soon.

I talked to Jonathon as we waited for Frank, and just explained that a nice man was going to come over and talk to us, and that he should feel free to tell the man whatever he was thinking. Jonathon looked at me with his big, brown eyes, and asked "Is he a BLACK man or a WHITE man?" I told him that I was not sure, but that I had talked to him on the phone and knew that he was a NICE man.

Frank arrived (he turned out to be a white man) and we visited for a few minutes. Jonathon was a bit uncomfortable, and went downstairs. He stated that he would just watch a video while we visited. I followed him down, and he insisted that he would not come up and talk. I found a neat Star Wars bank of Joshua's that Jonathon is not usually allowed to play with, and told him that as a special treat he could take it upstairs and show Frank how it worked. That was a good icebreaker, and upstairs we went.

Jonathon remained uncomfortable, and stood very close to me with the "Star Wars" bank. The first few questions that Frank asked Jonathon were ignored. Then Jonathon found a way to answer. After the question,

Jonathon would push the button on the bank, starting the "Star Wars" music. Under cover of the music, Jonathon would answer the question. When the music stopped, Jonathon stopped.

After answering a few non-threatening questions this way, Jonathon decided to sit down next to me. Two more questions were asked. "How long have you been at this house, Jonathon?" Jonathon's response was, "Awhile." The next question was "What do you think about living here? Do you like it?" Jonathon's answer was, to me, chilling. "Yeah, it's great. They love me, and nobody hurts me."

At this point, Jonathon decided to take a therapy position. I watched, in amazement, as my little boy decided to lie down with his head towards Frank and his legs over my lap. He answered the rest of the questions from this position. He shared openly, and his stories were consistent with what he has said in the past to us and to Jon. When asked for details about the 'licking pee' incident, Jonathon supplied them freely and quickly. He identified the location of the bathroom (upstairs, in the hall) and other details without any pause.

The remainder of the day was pure torture. Jonathon constantly pushed the limits, and was almost begging to have holding time. I must have held him (seemingly against his will, although his behavior was clearly requesting it) about a dozen times. Every time I held him, he leaned his face into my chest and cried buckets of tears. He had so much emotion to release, and I think that was the only way he knew to do it. He thrashed and fought while he cried, and then each time he would settle down and just continue with the crying. I held him, rocked him, and hugged him. It was a tough day for the little guy.

Wednesday we went to see a psychologist for an assessment. I was not sure how well Jonathon would do, given what he had already been through during the week. But the apointment had been made long ago, so I kept it. I am so glad I did! The psychologist was wonderful, and both Jonathon and I were very comfortable with him. He did a thorough evaluation, and Jonathon was very cooperative and attentive. I have never seen him work so hard. His concentration was incredible, and he gave full attention to the task at hand. He finished everything in one sitting, which is a great chore for any child! He clearly enjoyed himself. As we were leaving, he looked up into my eyes and said words I will never forget. "Thanks for bringing me, Mom. I did a really good job. I didn't know I could do all that stuff! I'm smart, aren't I?" He was clearly amazed at his abilities. His school experiences have been so negative that I think he came away from them with a feeling of inability and failure. Now he sees himself performing well, and he begins to question his feelings of inability! What a thrilling revelation he had! He is smart and capable, and he just never knew! He was on cloud nine for the rest of the day.

Lori

June 10, 2001

Dear Lori,

I'll have to delay a bit longer a reply to your last message. It's been quite a week, here. My son, Tom, has been in some sorrow about the departure this morning of his best buddy, who is moving to Washington. We are in the midst of some changes at my Institute that have required an enormous amount of my attention (up late every night at the computer, etc.), and I had to fire someone today (something I'm not particularly good at, and had delayed for several days, in an effort to protect her dignity). We tried to have our last campfire together tonight (until autumn); naturally, the wood was so soaked that we got mostly smoke. An apt metaphor, it seemed. All in all, a strange several days.

Of all astonishing things, I saw (as patients) an adolescent girl and her father this week, who were at each other's throats. Each complained bitterly about the other, but neglected to mention—until I gradually picked up on it—that the girl was about to go to California for the summer, to live with her mother. They had not thought to acknowledge it to each other. It was just going to happen, on the heels of their expressing their sorrow over it by tearing at each other. I asked them how they got so good at NOT seeing—much less tripping over—the elephant in the middle of the room. The girl fell silent, then began to cry, all the while leaning far over on the couch, away from her father. I thought I would have to physically push him towards her, but he finally caught my hints, moved over, pulled her in, and then the gusher really broke loose in her. She wailed about not wanting her parents to be divorced, but feeling guilty about that because she saw how much happier they were. She didn't want to leave dad, but felt guilty about THAT because then it looked as if she didn't want to be with her mom. Dad was a wonderful listener, and just let her cry and talk. I felt blessed (that I knew just what to do), but also astonished at the parallel. God does weird stuff.

Anyway, I will be out of commission until next week.
Michael

June 12, 2001

Michael,

Jonathon continues to insist that he was never a baby. He did not come out of anyone's tummy, and was never younger than three. We look at baby pictures, at home and at therapy, and he just looks. He understands the concept of babies and birth moms, but he just never was one. We do not have any baby pictures of him, but I have asked the agency to try to locate some.

Initially, Jonathon just refused to discuss the fact that he could have been a baby once. Now he is at the stage where he states that he wishes he could have been one. He wanted to be a baby, but nobody ever let him be their baby. He cries, and is wistful. If only someone would have let him be a baby, he could be like everyone else who came out of somebody's tummy.

Jon suggested that we try allowing him some baby time here. We tried that a couple of months ago, and the idea bombed. Jonathon refused to cuddle and drink from a bottle, and treated the whole idea with disdain. We tried again last night, and he was very receptive. I wrapped him up in a soft blanket, rocked him in the rocking chair, and fed him a bottle. Everyone else was in bed or other parts of the house, and it was just the two of us. He cuddled, and drank the bottle, and did goo-goos and gaa-gaas. It was a little bit awkward for him, and a couple of times he left the baby role, became big Jonathon again, and told me how to do something: "Hold the bottle like this," or, "Let Giggie be a baby, too".

Feel like a laugh about someone else's crazy times? Friday morning was supposed to be the final time of testing for my homeschoolers. We were about an hour into the testing, Jonathon was happily occupied, and all was well. I was working with Patrick and Maggie, and Rebecca was upstairs in the bathroom. Suddenly she was shouting, "Mom, come quick." The toilet had overflowed, and she did not know how to turn the water off. There was an inch of water (soiled water, that is) on the bathroom floor and into the hall. I turned the water off, and began the process of cleaning it up. About this time, Patrick yelled, "Mom, the water from the bathroom is leaking down into the kitchen." After getting the bathroom under control, I went downstairs to see how bad it was. I had to use pails, and remove the light fixture from the ceiling in order to drain the water. Quite a mess!

After a break of approximately an hour (for cleanup) we got back to testing. Concentration was not there, and we could not finish. The rest of the day was just full of frustrating little things. Nothing major, but not a great day. By evening, I wanted a break.

About 11:00 I invited my husband out for dessert. We went out to a local coffee shop, and had a quiet hour—too quiet, since we had left the cell phone in the car. When we got back in the car, there was a message from Maggie. "Mom, Dad, I think you should come home. The microwave is on fire. There is a ton of smoke, and we can't breathe." We immediately called, and nobody answered. We had visions of fire trucks, frightened children... We came home to a peaceful, but smelly, house. It seems that Patrick had a strained muscle, and decided to put the cherry pit pack into the microwave. It is (was) a great heat pack. After heating it in the microwave for 30-45 seconds, it stays warm for a long time and is a great help for sore muscles. Patrick forgot how long it was supposed to be heated, and placed it in the microwave for 11 minutes. Did you know that after that long, cherry pits burst, catch fire, and destroy microwaves? They also have a strong odor. So we aired out the house, started scrubbing and spraying and cleaning, and got to bed by 2:00 or so.

Friday was just one of those days.

At least I did not have to fire anybody. Actually, I kind of wanted to, but nobody here is fireable. They are all permanent fixtures, whether I like it or not! I will just have to adjust.

Lori

June 12, 2001

Dear Lori,

You were right. I did get something from hearing about your Friday. Are you sure all that stuff actually happened—in ONE DAY? Sounds like an Erma Bombeck column. I gather you are NOT making the interpretation that God (or one of her smirking cohorts) was getting you back for DARING to have a few moments alone with Paul, at the coffee shop?

Amazing about Jonathon and his readiness, now, to be a baby. Sure does prove the point that no therapy works for all, and no therapy works even for one child, at any given moment, but might work later. How many times has a child missed getting what he needed because the therapist or parent or other said, "We already tried that. It didn't work." You waited, tried some more, imagined that he might signal when he was ready, and you broke through.

Also amazing that he is rejecting the notion that he was ever a baby. BOY, does that make sense! Why in the world would he want to claim that time? With your help, perhaps he will, someday...

Michael

June 13, 2001

Michael,

Paul and I just returned from having dinner with a gentleman who wishes to act as a mentor for our little Jonathon. We are excited about the opportunity. His name is Spencer Bartley, and he has a non-profit organization to work with special needs and at-risk children. He is a wonderful man, and African-American, to boot.

We met Spencer months ago, at Taco Bell, where he works. (This is my very favorite restaurant, by the way—which ought to tell you plenty about the high-class life we are currently living!) Anyway, I'm so pleased to have him in our lives. For Jonathon to have an African-American man as a role model and friend can only be great for him.

While Paul and I were out, Jonathon had his "baby time" with Rebecca. It seems to have gone well. I love it that Jonathon is now willing to embrace the cuddling and nurturing that a mommy gives to her baby. Interestingly, Jonathon wet his bed last night for the first time in months. Coincidence? Part of the baby process? It does not really matter, but I'm curious to see if he wets the bed again tonight. I am very thankful to live in the days of such things as washing machines and dryers.

I found a book full of naked newborns, and bought it. Jonathon and I will have to spend some time looking at it. He's making great progress! Our most difficult times right now are the transitions from asleep to awake, and awake back to asleep.

Think I will go make the transition to asleep myself. I am a tired mommy.

Lori

June 17, 2001

Michael,

Happy Father's Day! Hope you and your family are celebrating in style.

Did you know that parenting is the most rewarding, frustrating, awe-inspiring, terror-inducing, smile-creating, gut-wrenching job in the whole world? It is the job that requires more of a person than anything else imaginable, yet it is a "no experience required" job. I cannot imagine NOT being a mother, yet I am not always sure that I will survive. I sure am thankful that we have a great dad/husband in this home to share the load, to partner in this wonderful job with me, and to be the one who sees the bright side when I am not so sure if the sun will shine again.

This has been a good, but sometimes frustrating, week. Jonathon's progress continues, with a few bumps in the road. I am having trouble discerning when Jonathon is manipulating vs. being truly needy.

A perfect example is our "baby time". This week we have had this special time on five occasions. The first time, Jonathon was a little awkward, but seemed ready for it. Once he settled in, we had some good eye contact and seemed to connect for a few seconds at a time. The second time we tried to have our baby time, Jonathon settled in a little easier, but I did not feel as much connection. By last night, which was baby time #4, Jonathon was not going to be a baby. He wanted the bottle, and the time and attention, but had no interest in anyone but him calling the shots. Just before the bottle, Jonathon had asked Paul for some cereal for his bedtime snack. I was in another room, but heard the conversation. Paul explained that we had just enough cereal for the morning, and gave the boys a different bedtime snack, which they ate. Jonathon had no idea that I had heard that conversation. As he settled into my arms for his bottle, he announced that babies really liked cereal, and that he should have cereal for his baby time on that night. When I told him that we were not going to have cereal, he looked away in a pout and stated that he would not be drinking his bottle. I told him that was fine, and set the bottle down. I started rocking him, and said that sometimes babies do not need to eat, but just need to be held and loved. He became angry and started kicking. I held him in a position so that he could not continue to kick, but kept rocking him and trying to soothe him. He did settle down, and decided in a few minutes that he would like to have the bottle, after all.

I felt like the whole cereal episode was Jonathon trying to manipulate our baby time, and he really fought any closeness when he did take the bottle. Tonight was baby time #5. Jonathon was not good at making eye contact, but spent a lot of time snuggling his face into my chest and pretending to sleep. I rocked him in that position. After we were done, Paul tucked him into his bed, which Jonathon called a crib. These baby times can be very special, and I am hopeful that they will be fruitful. I have to figure out the right combination of spontaneity and control, in order to keep these sessions positive. I want to look forward to having this be a time of sharing with Jonathon, rather than allow it to become a testing of wills.

Today I had another of those wondrous chances to watch my sons playing in a sprinkler and looking for all the world like a couple of regular boys. Jonathon's play tends to still be parallel rather than interactive, but the small amount of interaction that does occur is positive.

Paul and I appreciate the information that you sent to us, and both read it. The article on Theraplay gave us some ideas. Jonathon will love the "punching through the newspaper" game. He loves active games that require a lot of large motor activity. It is after such times that we seem to have the easiest time settling him down for hugs and affection.

Paul and I were in a bookstore this weekend, and I picked up the latest *Parenting* magazine. It caught my attention since the cover article is "Bonding with your Baby". I see attachment issues and bonding tips everywhere. Has it always been there, and I am just noticing it now? Or is the whole attachment concept just starting to be accepted and noticed and talked about in a bigger way?

I mailed off some photos of Jonathon to you. I thought you would like to see this child that we have been talking about for the past five months.

Lori

June 18, 2001

Lori,

Your thoughts about the difference between manipulation and being needy were certainly poignant. This is an age-old dilemma with all of us (parents), of course. Truth probably is that babies and toddlers DO do some things that could be understood as manipulation, as they attempt to teach us what they need, as they attempt to negotiate their way through dependence to independence to interdependence and mastery. The episodes of "babying" you described could be understood as highly compressed developmental episodes, in which Jonathon moved back and forth (as he is able to do, because he is not an actual baby) between developmental stages, and then tried to mix and match (being little and needy; being big and independent; being big and needy but not too much and wouldn't it be nice to be held and be small and have no responsibilities and still be in charge of everything?!). He may, in other words, be quite unable to remain just one age while he is being held. He may be trying out developmental sequences on you, trying to learn about fluid movement amongst stages, trying to learn about mastery, trying to learn about boundaries.

My best,
Michael

June 20, 2001

Michael,

Jonathon wakes up slowly in the morning, and the first few minutes are pleasant. He likes to be held, and is gentle. That lasts about 5 minutes. Then he wakes up, and transforms. Mornings, right after he really wakes up, are not good times for Jonathon. He is very aggressive, as if it has been pent up all night and needs to be released. Then he starts his "bad word" vocabulary, and gets out of control easily. I am trying to figure out a new way to do mornings that might be an easier transition for him. He might need something very physical before he tries to settle down to eat breakfast and start his day. My first thought was to have him do some trampoline jumping, but I think that would be too stimulating. I have tried hard hugs/wrestling and that has not done the trick. I will keep trying until we find something that works. Trial and error. That seems to be the key. Keep trying until something works.

Summer has begun, with lots of play time for Jonathon and James. This will be a summer to remember, I am sure. No big plans, other than a possible road trip to see the Hope for the Children community in Illinois, to get ideas. If we make the trip, it will be Lindsay, Siobhan, Jonathon, James, Maggie, and me. We see things moving into place to start getting serious about having such a community here, so we need to get out there and check it out. We are off to a play date with friends.

Lori

June 21, 2001

Dear Lori,

Your description of the two stages of Jonathon's awakening in the mornings makes me wonder if his aggressiveness, in the second stage, might connect to birth. Do you know anything about the exact circumstances of his birth? (If you have told me about these things before, and I forgot, please forgive me.) Were drugs used during the delivery? Was he breech? Was the cord wrapped?

There's something about the way you described it that made me wonder if he had been pinned down *in utero*—mechanically (by some sort of pressure, the cord, or being stuck in the birth canal), or due to drugs (illicit or prescribed) taken by mom—in a way that he "recovered" from suddenly, with a primitive lunge toward air, breath, light, space, an opening. He could be re-experiencing the relative calm of intrauterine life during sleep, then reacting suddenly and primitively to the coming of morning (light), as if he has to fight his way out, or has to fight to survive, or just has to fight for himself. If you've ever seen a newborn react violently to being unwrapped from a blanket (hands and arms suddenly flung outward, terrified look on the face, screaming—only helped by tight swaddling), contemplate whether there seems to be any connection.

If this is the case, he might be helped by "squishing" (wrapping him in blankets, then applying pressure by lying on top of him, slowly releasing the weight/pressure and unfolding him); by holding and soothing (tho' this might be antithetical to his feelings of panic and the desperate need to fight something off, to survive).

It could also be a reaction to another kind of very similar trauma—something about being contained and having to get out, or something that happened while he slept and which he discovered upon awakening.

I just suspect that his wonderful body is a placard on which is displayed his story and his feelings.

Michael

June 22, 2001

Michael,

Your insights, as usual, give me much to think about and something to try.

I do not know much about Jonathon's birth. "Normal vaginal delivery" is all that is written. I know that the birth was not gleefully anticipated, and that birth mom did not care to birth, or parent, her baby. I also know that, although no illegal drugs were reported at birth, his brain waves (according to one doctor's report) show signs of drug exposure *in utero*.

Regardless of possible birth trauma, I believe it is very likely that Jonathon experienced other "awakening" traumas. The thought of being placed in a closed container, and fighting to get out, seems consistent with the abuse of his past. Or the idea that he could have been awakened from a sleeping state to some sort of abuse is also very possible.

Jonathon's pattern in the morning indicates that you are probably right. The five or ten minutes of peace that I referred to are very much like the pre-awake state of a newborn. He gets out of bed, or cries out from his bed, and wants to cuddle. His eyes remain closed, and his suckling reflex is strong. His voice is soft and pleading. The transition from this state to his aggressive state is amazing. One minute he is cuddling, and suddenly he is loud and aggressive and demanding. He screams, yells bad words, and is physically out of control. Thrashing, kicking, jumping. Completely out of control.

This morning I tried your suggestion of squishing. Jonathon called to me from his room, and I went in for our morning hugs. I cuddled him tight, which is our normal routine, as he started to wake up. He did his regular suckling noises, eyes closed and all. I gently rocked him, and talked to him quietly. As he started to come to his awakened state, I wrapped him in his blanket, and squished him hard against me. I continued to rock gently in his bed, and talk softly to him. "Good morning, precious boy. Mommy loves you. I am glad you are waking up. I wanted to see you." (That is pretty much the dialogue every morning. The "I am glad you are waking up" part is as much for me as it is for him. I must admit that it was becoming difficult to joyfully anticipate his awakening when mornings kept being so challenging.) As Jonathon became aware of being awake, he looked up and said "Mom, you are squishing me." I replied that yes, I was squishing, but I would be careful to squish without hurting. Jonathon was okay with that. I continued this for about twenty minutes, and then began to release him. After another ten minutes or so, Jonathon was fully released. At that point we went downstairs for breakfast and medicine. Jonathon kept control much better than usual, and breakfast had no traumatic episodes. Jonathon was fidgety, and not terribly cooperative, but not completely out of control. After we ate, he wanted to help me clean up. We scrubbed cabinets, and he had a great time being my special assistant. I figured that was probably a good release of energies for him. All in all, it was a good morning routine. I will let you know if it continues.

Lori

June 23, 2001

Dear Lori,

I'm amazed at your willingness to put 30 minutes into this, especially early in the morning, when there must be a great many demands on your energy (not to mention your own, internal urgency to get going, to get the day moving). I certainly do "get" your meaning, about beginning to not anticipate his awakening with much pleasure.

It's impossible to know, I suspect, what the culprits are. Having worked with a few folks during regressions, I now appreciate the utter panic that the newborn (or pre-born) can feel about being born, especially when drugs are interfering, for example, with the use of the lower body; or when the cord is making movements and escape attempts counter-productive; or when the toxic marinade of the mother's body is communicating so profoundly *her* fear, or rage, or dread. (Social referencing research—never applied to newborns or prenates, to my knowledge—teaches us that the mother's attitude, facial expression, etc. communicates profoundly to the baby, and guides the baby to fear, welcome, wariness, etc.)

I have to tell you that I am also surprised that Jonathon just took note of the fact that you were squishing, and let you do it, for 20 minutes. Either there is a *huge* level of trust, or it filled a need, or both.

My best,
Michael

June 23, 2001

Michael,

Jonathon woke up this morning, quietly, and crawled into bed with me. He did the normal "curled up, cuddly time", with his right arm wrapped around me, and the left hand caressing my arm. He was very quiet, with his mouth and tongue doing the "suckling" thing. As he began to really wake up, he started to act distressed and anxious. I wrapped around him, with him wrapped in my blanket, and held him tight. He calmed back down, and resumed the suckling noise. His eyes closed again, and he was peaceful. After about 15 minutes, I had to use the bathroom. Paul had walked into the room and I asked him to trade places with me. Jonathon responded poorly. He begged me to stay, and said that he needed my nightgown. I offered to change clothes, and to let him hold my nightgown. He said that he really needed to have the person inside. I was amazed and amused. And touched. But I still really needed to use the bathroom! So Paul and I did change places. Jonathon was a bit silly for a few minutes, and then calmed back down. He and Paul ended up telling stories to each other, and they had a nice time together. Then we all went downstairs for breakfast, and Jonathon was a happy boy.

Just wanted you to know that the second day of our new morning routine worked well, and I think we are on to something good! Thanks for your suggestions, insights, knowledge...

Lori

June 24, 2001

Dear Lori,

Please don't ever forget (I know you won't) the story about his needing your nightgown (what a clever ruse, to avoid it appearing that he was too needy of human connection!), converted, when challenged, to his needing, "...the person inside". I am astounded that he would acknowledge this. This is more than progress. This is a shift in character...

Michael

June 25, 2001

Michael,

You commented on my willingness to put 30 minutes into our new morning routine, trying to find a better way for Jonathon to wake up without trauma, aggression, etc. I have found, through many years of parenting, that time spent proactively is usually a great investment. The time, energy, and frustration spent when reacting is much greater and takes much more out of the day, and a greater toll on the mom! And that is not even counting how much better the day goes for the child, if he can be guided BEFORE he gets out of control, rather than living with the consequences of being out of control. Of course, you know all of this. I just state it here so that you know why I am willing to spend the time. It is for my own selfish good.

This same decision to try to parent proactively is why I take the time to home school some of my children, and why I believe therapy is worth the time and financial investment. And why I take my children out on dates. I do it because I love my children, but I also do it because I do not want to pay the consequences of NOT doing it! My motives are not 100% selfless.

Along these same lines, I have already realized that too much free time is not a good thing for little boys or girls. I have just initiated a schedule for our summer days, which allows no more than 30 minutes of totally free play at a time for Jonathon and James. The day is broken down into half-hour blocks, and has quiet times, times with Mom, workbook times, etc., all interspersed into the day. My goal is to keep Jonathon close at hand, and monitored carefully, without making him feel as if he is not being allowed to have a good summer. All of the activities will be positive and fun, but most will be supervised. Actually, all will be supervised. Most will include direct adult (or older sibling) involvement.

I have had a nice surprise added to our summer. Robin, Joshua's very wonderful girlfriend, will be moving down here on July 1st. She will be my mother's helper for the next several months, which will help us achieve what we need in the near future. My house has taken a serious toll since Jonathon arrived, and we are all trying to keep things under control. But there are only so many hours in the day, and 24 do not seem to be enough. It will be a God-send to have Robin here. She will be living with some good friends of ours, just a couple of miles away. I will include her in some of Jonathon's therapy, and she will be a great help to me.

Lori

June 26, 2001

Dear Lori,

You might guess at how many thousands of hours I have spent, in the past 33 years, trying to suggest this notion of proactive, child-centered investment as a clever and selfish act! There's nothing clean and altruistic about learning what a train sounds like as it comes toward you, and deciding that self-interest is, indeed, served by getting organized, thinking things out, and taking action that will help one avoid being pulverized. Well put.

Michael

June 27, 2001

Michael,

Jonathon and I had the longest night last night. He is sick, and ran a high fever yesterday and through the night. I was checking on him about midnight, and his fever was back up to 103. As I felt his head, he opened his eyes, and said, "Mommy, I need you. Please cuddle me." Needless to say, I gave him more Motrin and a drink, and then we cuddled. He woke up frequently through the night, and made contact with me each time. "Mommy, hold me." "Mommy, I love you." It felt SO good to be able to comfort him, and for it to mean something to him.

Two of his wake-ups were more remarkable than the others. Once he woke up and needed to use the bathroom. He got up, walked straight to his closet, and began to pull down his pants. I was able to get him to the bathroom, but he clearly would have preferred to just do his business right there in the closet. I have found urine in that closet a few times, and suspected that something was happening in the night. I was not sure if it was purposeful, or done in a sleepy stupor. (Twice in the last day he has purposely urinated in the house, on the floor. He has hit the living room carpet, and the family room all over the place. If you include the bedroom closet, he has managed to hit each of the three levels of the house.)

The second episode occurred after a bad dream. Jonathon woke up, and told me that he was scared. He was shaking, and told me that a skeleton was chasing him, and he thought it was going to get him. I held him, and reassured him that the skeleton was not real, and that he had just been dreaming. He calmed down, and then stated that he was not scared anymore. I was glad that I had been able to comfort him, and I asked him what helped him to not be scared anymore. He answered with this profound statement: "I am not scared anymore because now no one can hurt me, and I live with you." Maybe the skeleton that had been chasing him in his dream WAS real, and maybe we are making it go away.

I get so excited about these wonderful times! I am not happy that Jonathon is sick, but I am thrilled with the opportunities we received as a result. I would not trade last night for anything, except maybe a chance to go back and be there for Jonathon in his infancy.

I am thrilled that Lindsay saw you at Christmas, as you were fresh on her mind when a little surprise package with RAD arrived in our home in January. If she had not connected us with you, I really do not think we would be where we are with our Jonathon. I have said it before, and I will say it again: We need every bit of the support system that we have in place. Without you, Jon, our circle of understanding friends (which is smaller than our past circle of friends) and the books that we have read, etc, we would not have survived the first couple of months. There is no chance that we would have moved into adoption without every ounce of good fortune that was heaped upon us. We are so thankful. So I know that Lindsay had to see you so that she could encourage us, and lead us to you.

Lori

June 27, 2001

Dear Lori,

You have a marvelous way of taking life as it comes, and of finding meaning in it, HOWEVER it comes. It took me many years of [pseudo-] adulthood to even begin to approach life that way. When I did, it was my grandparents (long ago deceased) that led me. Their spiritual influence and example came back to me when I needed it MANY years later. (No wonder I have such faith in the potential for influencing children's lives— even when the results of such influence are not evident right away, or even for many years.)

So, things "click" for you. Stuff has meaning. Life goes someplace, even when you can't tell where. And when you can't, you are willing to hold on, knowing that the ride is not without purpose, and maybe even not without direction. This is how "random" events and coincidences become non-random and non-accidental elements in a larger whole. And this is how sitting up all night with a sick kid becomes a treasure.

Amazing…

Michael

June 29, 2001

Michael,

I just returned from speaking as part of a panel on home schooling. I was surrounded by people who think much like we do, and who have decided to take very active roles in the lives of their children. It was refreshing, and I did not stick out as "weird" there. Or at least not as REALLY weird. I do have more children than the other panelists, but maybe they aren't done adding to their families yet. And I do have a more diverse group than the others, but that just means that our family pictures will be more colorful.

Jonathon is really enjoying our morning "hard hugs". He is responding nicely on the mornings that we spend a good amount of time holding
him tightly, releasing him gradually, and allowing him to transition into
the day slowly. Today he woke up while I was downstairs, and I did not
realize that he was awake until he came to find me in the kitchen. He
wanted to eat, so I gave him some hugs, and then fed him. He started acting silly (saying bad words like "stupid" and "shut-up") and then got very
loud and rude. I sat down next to him, and told him that he needed to
stop saying bad words. He looked right at me and said, "I guess I need
consequences. You will have to hold me now." I agreed that he needed
holding time, and suggested that we head to the rocking chair. Jonathon
told me that that was a bad idea, and that what we needed was the holding that we do in the mornings, when I hold him tight in a blanket while
he is laying down. He missed our new routine, and found a way to work
into it. Such a clever boy!

Lori

June 30, 2003

Michael,

Thought I would send a quick Saturday morning note to let you
know how wonderful life is with our little tribe over here.

Jonathon and James are dressed as twins (sometimes moms have to do
things to humor themselves, regardless of any meaning to the children)
and look adorable. They are both here in the room with me. Jonathon is
building a boat, and James is "reading" a book. Both are very involved in
their activities, at least for the moment.

Downstairs, my new aquarium is set up, the water is in, and we are
almost ready for the fish. The aquarium is a late Christmas gift to me. On
Christmas, Paul gave me a certificate promising me a china cabinet of my
choice. I have wanted a bowed-front china cabinet for years. My plan was
to display Grandma's china in it. We started looking around antique
shops, getting ideas. Then Jonathon came, in January. I put the idea on
hold for a bit. As life progressed, I realized that this is not the right time

in my life for a china cabinet. I would be tense if someone happened to throw something in the dining room (between Jonathon and James, I cannot imagine that NOT happening) and upset if the cabinet broke. I would not be able to replace Grandma's china if it broke. I would be sad, not because of any big need to have china, but because of the sentimental value. So, I decided against a china cabinet. In it's place, I got a steam cleaner for the carpets (quite a necessary item with carpets, six children, two dogs, one day-care dog, and children with allergies) and an aquarium. Fish are so peaceful to watch, and I cannot imagine a better thing for Jonathon. I think all the children will enjoy it. The aquarium is plexiglass, by the way. Unbreakable. In this house, that means "more difficult to break".

I realized how much I adore this newest child when I had a disagreement with my mom this week. I share almost everything with her, which is maybe a bit too much. I told her about the choking episode (when I caught Jonathon trying to choke James), and her comment was "Are you sure you know what you are doing? Is keeping Jonathon the right thing?" She meant well. She does not know Jonathon, and she does know and love James. I know she loves Jonathon in theory, but she could not have a big attachment to him yet, since she has not met him. Therefore, her comment was not unreasonable. But Jonathon is one of my six children. He is as much mine as any of them, and I would never consider anything other than working through his problems. (That is not to say that I cannot understand the anguishing decision that some people must make because their RAD children are really dangerous, and need to be placed elsewhere for their safety.) Jonathon is completely ours, and his issues are not too difficult. Anyway, life with our boy, and all of our children, is good.

Lori

July 1, 2001

Dear Lori,

If you are ever invited to speak to other parents about life with a child with RAD, you've got to be sure to tell the bowed china cabinet story. It's a classic. A STEAM CLEANER FOR THE CARPET!! I mean, REALLY! Good that Paul didn't actually bring home a carpet cleaner for your Christmas present, in the first place, eh?

And so there are those "just right" days when kids are, well, sort of REGULAR: fun, interesting, cute, not lighting anything on fire at the moment, or peeing onto a pile of clothes in the closet.

Fish tank, eh? Had you thought about becoming a den mother or taking in laundry, just to keep you from not having enough things to attend to?

Michael

July 1, 2001

Dear Michael,

One of the things I love about Paul is that he is sweet enough to want to get me a china cabinet, and flexible enough to see my point about the steam-cleaner/aquarium substitution. You are right about it being a good thing that he did not buy me a steam-cleaner as my Christmas present. Thinking about the china cabinet WAS much more romantic.

Speaking of flexibility: it is a good thing. I cannot imagine being very rigid and still enjoying parenting, especially with a child like Jonathon. I recently spoke to a small group of parents about flexibility in reference to schooling. In my talk, one of my points was that to be flexible with some-thing means that the something must exist. One cannot be flexible with their schedule if no schedule exists in the first place. I see too many peo-ple saying that they are "flexible", when what they really mean is that they have no plan. "Flexible" does not mean "lack of a plan". Parents need a parenting plan, complete with goals for their children, ideas about disci-pline, etc. Once a plan is in place, if there is a need for change, then the need can be met. Goals can be altered, dreams can be re-worked. But there still needs to be a firm foundation on which to build, and a secure base where the child feels safe.

My number one goal for each of my children is that they reach adulthood as people who love God, love their fellow man, and do their best to be positive members of society. Each child must, with our help, evaluate his God-given talents, and then use them to their full potential.

I often visited a Burger King, where a sweet man named Tom worked. Tom had Downs Syndrome. He had a strong passion for life, and greeted each day with gusto. I never visited that Burger King without having my spirits lifted. Tom would greet me, tell me he loved me, hand me a straw for my drink, and share stories about his family and his life. He always had a smile and something sweet to say.

I once went to see a doctor. I was referred to him because he was so knowledgeable in his field. He must have had a fight with his wife that morning, and he was grumpy. He spent no time trying to figure out what was wrong with me, and seemed very distracted and unhappy. I left his office feeling very sorry for him. He did not strike me as a nice person.

I think Tom's parents should be very proud of the fine job they did with their son. He makes a difference in lives, and is an inspiration to those around him. Success is a matter of perspective.

My children will know that flexibility is good, but that there are also absolutes and values from which we never stray. Good is always good, and evil is always evil. If we cannot get something done without compromising our integrity, then we do not get it done. The end DOES NOT justify the means.

How can I apply these thoughts to practical parenting? I try to meet the needs of the child, even if it means a china cabinet has to wait. I let them know that they are loved unconditionally. I am flexible enough to change my schedule when necessary. But lying will get consequences EVERY time, and destroying another's property will mean that you have to help Mommy pull weeds and miss some play time.

These are my thoughts for the day.
Lori

July 2, 2001,

Dear Lori,

Did we share grandparents? I don't think either of them ever said, out loud, any of the things you just said, but they lived it as clearly as you said it, and I learned it well.

You might be interested to know that the basic rules of therapy with children are similar to those you articulated about life around the house. A child is not allowed to hurt me, or to damage my stuff. After that, pretty much anything is OK. We won't negotiate about the two key things (hurting me or damaging my property), but we will negotiate as long as it is helpful about everything else, and the child is allowed to call many of the shots. Limits are still tested, but I actually think they are tested less (in the therapy room AND in the home) when they are very clear, to start with. I consider it trauma for a child to have to flail around in life, trying to understand limits and expectations that have never been enunciated (often in the name of flexibility).

Michael

July 3, 2001

Michael,

Did you know that I do not require a lot of sleep (which is a huge blessing)? I cannot imagine life without significant amounts of reading and writing, and I need some time to myself each day. To keep up with the children, make any progress with Jonathon and James, school some of them at home, and still read and write would be almost impossible if I needed to spend a lot of time sleeping, too. I do well on five or six hours, but if I get less I just need to catch up once a week or so.

Last night I returned home, late, after helping Robin move into her new place. When I arrived home, Jonathon was still awake, and wanting bottle time. (Rebecca had done the bedtime ritual with him, and he was in bed, but just could not sleep.) I cuddled him, and we talked and had a good LONG time together. About midnight, I left him, but wanted to stay awake and listen for him until I was sure he was sleeping soundly. I checked my emails, and there you were. I started writing, and when I was finished, Jonathon was snoring away. Perfect timing!

Lori

July 6, 2001

Michael,

Life's lessons are not always easily learned. This has been an educational week for me.

Did you know that Tiger Barbs and Guppies do not do well together? Did you know that if you bought fish from the Tetra family, and then bought Guppies, too, you would end up buying a second tank so that your Guppies would have a fighting chance? And then, most importantly, did you know that boys like to drink milk, but Guppies do not? So much for a fighting chance for the Guppies. We caught the "accident" quickly, and at this point only one pregnant mommy guppy bit the dust. We have changed the water twice, added a new filter, and hope to have some survivors at the end of it all.

It is possible, I believe, to have delayed reactions to life changes. For instance, if a child was to have some wild behavior a few weeks after an adoption announcement, rather than right away, it could still be in response to the announcement. Correct? If this has not been a wild week of testing the limits, my name is not George.

A few thoughts on consequences:

1. It is possible to have so many consequences lined up that it is impossible to keep track of them.
2. Consequences should probably be things that do not keep the child inside the house forever. When the child stays in, the mom must, too.
3. If a child is going to pull weeds as a consequence, Mom should stay close by. It is costly to replace all of the flowers.
4. Whenever possible, a consequence should be something that can be carried out on the day of the infraction. Each new day is best started as a truly NEW day, with fresh hope and possibilities.

We are looking at a used 15-passenger van today. My dream car. Who needs a sporty convertible? Or a sporty station wagon? That is all for this moment in time. Off to crowd children into the station wagon, to go look at the more spacious van.

Lori

July 8, 2001

Dear Lori,

Sounds as if Friday was one of those days when perspective was elusive, when sighing could be heard coming out of your body (and tears would have come, too, if the right person had put his/her arm around you at just the right moment), when you must have wondered if there was any space for just you.

I just watched "Baby" (Jean Stapleton and Farrah Fawcett). There's a line about what a huge risk the mother in the movie took (emotionally), to which another mom responded, "That's what mothers do." Exactly true. More than fathers, often. And surely more than anyone else, in nearly any risky venture. Moms are just hanging out there, day in and day out. The risk is not just that there will be death (from some terrible mistake or omission), but also that there will be life—and it will be impossible to understand, or will remind you every day that you should have done it a different way or should have made a different decision. And every day, you pick up again and do it some more, and you're still hanging out there. With risk there is possibility, of course; surely that must be part of the reason moms are willing to take it. But with risk there is also terror, and passion, and exhaustion (partly from the worry that it is all going wrong even as we speak) and the desperate attempt to see if YOU are still there on the other side, at the end. Except there also is no end, so when do you evaluate?

At least get a good radio in your van, with deep, warm speakers, for those days when you need to make the front, left seat a cocoon for just a few moments.

No, I didn't know about tragedy of the milk/guppy interface, as it were. But, then again, most folks don't.

Michael

July 8, 2001

Michael,

The funny thing is, I thought I had it in perfect perspective. Life was kind of stinky, and that was perspective enough.

The truth, of course, is that life is pretty darn good; some days are just more challenging than others.

The good thing is that I really LOVE my 15-passenger van. A good friend of mine previously owned it, and I always teased her that I really wanted her van. That was when she had 8 children, and I still fit fairly comfortably into the station wagon with my 5 children. The sixth child just pushed us over the top, and I suddenly felt a need for the bigger form of transportation.

This morning we went to church, and Jonathon made it through Sunday School AND Children's Church without any major difficulties. He was rewarded for his great job. We gave him a quick hug, and later in the day let him rent a video game.

Our video game rules are strict. No guns, swords, or violence of any kind. In fact, he is pretty much limited to sports games. Strict time limits, too. He loves to play the games, so it is a privilege that we allow in small doses. When he first came to us, he swore that he should play lots of games that we do not approve of. We had to cut out playing all together for a while, as he did not seem to be able to enjoy the tamer games that we allow. Now he does enjoy the sports games, and loves to compete with his parents and siblings. It has become a fairly positive time of interaction. He always beats me, and that is with me trying.

Lori

July 8, 2001

Dear Lori,

Boy, you move quickly! On Friday, it was "I'm going to go LOOK at a van." On Sunday night, it's a done deal. Guess mothering a small village doesn't leave extra time to shop around at length.

Of the things in Jeremy's life that we modified this year that had (we think) major impact, taking control of TV watching was in the top three or four. He had a long history of watching pretty much any time he wanted, for pretty much as long as he wanted. I could certainly feel the seductive pull of this particular way of dealing with Jeremy's behavior and strangeness, because it actually means not having to deal with Jeremy at all. It was also, of course, a direct match with his autism. He would obsess, rewinding a video over and over to re-watch a few seconds that particularly captured him. He would stare, get lost, and have a great opportunity to not interact with the family. It was difficult to rouse him while he was watching, and he was nearly always grouchy when asked to turn it off and come to have dinner or join the rest of us in some activity. It was non-human comfort, it asked nothing of him in return, and it demanded nothing of his brain except that it did not have to work, for a while.

He has not been at all happy about the change. He is allowed to watch a total of 2.5 hours per week, and he gets some choice about how to split that time up, etc. Oddly, there have been many weeks this past year when he watched far less than the allotted 2.5 hours (to our surprise).

In our family, this became part of a larger effort to help him get connected, and to be able to tolerate human interaction without "losing it". This means asking him (at the dinner table, for example) what someone just said; asking him (in the car, for example) to tell me about the scenery we just passed; looking at him (in church, for example) when he begins to do his finger autisms (which reminds him to be conscious, and to find something else to do with his body). He now feeds back to us that it is important to be "part of the family".

In any event (did I get carried away with telling you about our experience?), dealing with electronic stimulation is an incredibly important part of helping children like ours, and I am amazed at how frequently families will bring a child to me with serious attention (or even attachment) problems, who are quite unwilling to take the [relatively easy, it seems to me] first step of controlling the electronic stimulation to which the child is subjected. Now I'm preaching...

Michael

July 9, 2001

Michael,

I have usually thought things over (at least in concept) before I make a move. Therefore, when opportunity knocks, I can move forward with quick decisiveness. For instance, I have thought and prayed about parenting hard-to-place, special-needs children. It is not hard for me to want to move forward into foster/adopt situations when I have already made a general plan. When the right child is offered to us, we know it and can move forward. (With Jonathon, it was easy to move forward for foster care. The adoption part was a bit more difficult.)

We spend a lot of time in the car. As a matter of fact, we spend too much time in the car, for sports, therapy, piano, seeing friends. Therefore, the concept of, "We are too crowded in this car and need a bigger one" was deeply ingrained in my brain. When the right "bus" came along, it was time to make the move. Simple and straightforward.

All of that is to say that I am not terribly impulsive. Sometimes I think that I am. I love to remember the look on Paul's face when I introduced him to his new son (James) one night. That SEEMED impulsive. In fact, I would bet that MOST people would see it as impulsive to do volunteer work in an orphanage and just bring a son home one day. But it was not, upon close review, anything other than just the right and only decision open to me on that day.

Lori

July 9, 2001

Michael,

I wrote to you last night, and forgot half of what I meant to say. How does that happen?

I was glancing through *Parents Magazine* yesterday, and saw an article on dealing with race issues with children. I read it, and saw all the common sense ideas presented (be honest and open with the children, etc.). There were quotes from some parents, and I thought one of them was profound. It relates to much more than race issues, and I think it hits the nail on the head for all of our children. Here it is:

"I believe that his best defense is to know himself well, a person defined by the crevices of his own soul rather than parentage or looks." (Felicia Lee, "My Battle For My Son", *Parents Magazine*, July 2001)

Parentage matters, but parenting matters more. And if we can parent well enough that our children know their own souls, we have done a good job.

Jonathon had a nightmare last night, and woke up screaming in terror. He was quite upset, and allowed Paul to cuddle him and calm him back down. He woke up the whole family. While Paul comforted and calmed Jonathon, I did the same for James. Rebecca had to walk her dogs, who woke up and, therefore, needed to urinate. It was a middle-of-the-night zoo. Everyone did settle back down, and we were all sleeping soundly this morning when the alarm went off.

Lori

July 9, 2001

Dear Lori,

Did I ever mention "PACT: An Adoption Alliance" to you? They are an organization in San Francisco, dedicated to supporting families who have adopted children of color. They put out a newsletter. If interested, let me know and I will look up their address for you.

I can picture the nighttime zoo... so sorry. I know the lack of sleep and the ever-present fires that must be put out can begin to have a cumulative effect. Challenges one's perspective. What a blessing there are so many hands to take part in holding it all together.

Michael

July 9, 2001

Dear Michael,

In reference to the nighttime zoo: We all survived. In fact, those are the fun nights, to be remembered years from now. Kind of comical, after the fact.

About a year ago, a friend of mine offered to paint a mural on one of our basement walls. I took her up on her offer, as she is a good artist, and I loved the idea of a mural on this wall. She came over to survey the area, and get my ideas about what I would like to see on that wall. I pictured a calm, cottage scene: water, flowers, kind of a Thomas Kincaid look. She spent some time here, and gave me her impressions of what would work. The mural is great. It is a zoo. She, somehow, thought that was more appropriate in my home than the cottage scene. I have never understood that.

Lori

July 10, 2001

Michael,

I have long understood that my wishing/thinking/planning/visualizing personality does leave me at a handicap because I can become disappointed if/when things do not turn out the way I might have expected. For that reason, I make a concerted effort to plan options. For instance, when we moved to Korea, we really thought we were there to adopt a healthy baby girl. We had, however, discussed children with special needs, and their plight. We had determined that if we ever were to parent such a child, we would do certain things. There was that option already planned for, without really meaning to plan for it. So when the special little James came along, the plan was easy to call upon.

I keep that whole flexibility thing in mind as much as possible in life. None of us ever knows what tomorrow will bring, and what we will be called on to do. I want to be available to life.

The number one goal is always to raise Godly, loving children who are positive members of society. And for all of us to enjoy the process. That does not mean that every part of the process will be enjoyable. But all in all, life is.

Jonathon and James had swimming lessons today, and Jonathon is very proud of the very good job that he did. He listened and tried everything the teacher asked of him.

Lori

July 10, 2001

Dear Lori,

I've been curious for a long time about the connection between certain brain types, and the functioning of the people in whose heads those brains reside. Your thoughts about whether you are impulsive or have, actually, so thoroughly thought out—maybe even visually "lived" with an idea, in advance—that actually doing the idea is not impulsive at all, fit with my wonderings. Is the ability to visualize what a child (or a relationship, or a dinner, for that matter) could be like, if given the right stuff, a great aid in providing that "right stuff"? For some, does such visualization become a trap: for the child (who may or may not be able to live up to the visualization, consistently) or for the parent (who may be set up for disappointment, AND be unable to quickly shift gears to another goal, another visualization, because he/she is "stuck" on the original one)? Without the capacity to picture what one is after, it seems to me that organizing behavior (toward the goal) is vastly more difficult. Unless you've already "lived" in the 15-passenger van many times in your head, seen what problems it solves, played out what it would be like to see it in the driveway or park it somewhere, then the decision about whether or not to buy one that suddenly presents itself is complicated, full of angst and second-guessing. I'd like to think about this more, with particular respect to fostering, and making the decision to adopt.

Michael

July 12, 2001

Michael,

Yesterday I ran into an old friend, whom I had not seen in months. We had the normal, "Hi, how are you? What's new in your home?" conversation. How in the world do you describe "what's new" in a short conversation with someone who has not met or heard anything about Jonathon?

Option #1: I was tired, so I could have complained a bit, and played the martyr role. Something like this: "We have this very difficult new child who has been abused in his past, and we are in the process of adopting him. It has been very challenging, but SOMEONE needs to take care of him, and it might as well be us."

Option#2: I could have been extremely open and truthful. "In January we took custody of a new foster child. It has been the most difficult time of our lives. We have been to the edge of insanity and back about a million times. He has Reactive Attachment Disorder, and relationships are not comfortable or easy for him. He has pushed every button we have, and tested every limit. Many of our belongings have seen better days, and so have we. I have been bruised, scratched, kicked, and spit upon. This child has caused friction between Paul and I, and there was no peace in our home for weeks or months. We got to a point where we did not think we could handle another day, and were not sure what to do. We came really close to calling the social workers and telling them that enough was enough. Instead, we decided to adopt him. Many of our friends think we are crazy, and we are not so sure about that, ourselves. But our child is making progress, and we have completely fallen in love with him. He needs our family, and our family would not be complete without him. He is working hard with a great therapist, and we have a wonderful support system in place. Our lives have changed dramatically, but the process of parenting this new child is getting more comfortable each day. That is what we have been doing. How about you?"

I did not choose option #1 *or* 2. I chose a much easier #3. In response to "What's new?"

I simply replied, "Oh, not too much. We are in the process of adopting our newest foster son. He is a sweet boy. Other than that, things around our house are about the same. How about you?"

It is just not possible to share all that we have been through in the past six months. It has been a wild ride!

Lori

July 16, 2001

Dear Lori,

Fern Kupfer, author of *Before and After Zacharia*, and the mother of a severely disabled child, writes about how SHE began to answer people when they merely asked, "How are you?" She describes the stunned looks on people's faces when she actually TOLD them!

I can imagine the dilemma. Do people want to know, really? Is a truthful response a conversation-stopper or an intimacy-producer? Do we really want people to feel as helpless as we do? Do we want people to just leave us alone, or do we want to wipe the smug looks from their faces? Do we want affirmation that we made a wise decision—or, at least, an heroic one, or a wondrous one? Do we fear the judgments they are making of us, even as we speak, or do we, frankly, not care anymore, about a decision we made in the dark of the night and in fear and in hope and with faith but with way more than just quivers?

I will be off-line for about 10 days. I will look forward to continuing to witness the saga, and to, occasionally, try to support you and Paul a little.

My best...
Michael

July 16, 2001

Michael,

I will have to look at *Before and After Zacharia* to get better ideas on answering questions that people ask. I am sure that the innocent asker of the "How are you?" question does not expect the kinds of answers that we are capable of giving.

We have a new diagnosis for Jonathon. Paul and I have decided that he suffers from Chronic Disobedience. (Chronic: of long duration; continuing; constant, subject to habit.)

Siobhan and I have an appointment in Rantoul, Illinois on August 22nd. We have wanted to get there for so long, and hope to start a community here, so we are very excited about the opportunity to finally see "Generations of Hope" in person.

Will you and Mary be around during that week? We would love to meet you, if the timing is right.

We are trying to make some decisions about the trip. I don't know how many of us will travel. There is part of me that wants to bring the youngest four children (Patrick, Maggie, James, and Jonathon) with us. They would love to see what we are trying to do, and it would be fun to travel with them. Also, I do not relish the idea of leaving Jonathon behind. On the other hand, it will be harder to concentrate on the task at hand (meeting with Brenda Krause Eheart, the founder and director, with the children there. Back and forth I go, unable to make a firm decision. I am inclined to leave the children here, but the community is all about children, so it seems kind of natural to bring them. And the consequences I will pay for leaving Jonathon behind could be ugly. Within the next day or two, I will probably flip a coin and call it a decision. (I decide all important things that way.)

Lori

July 17, 2001

Dear Lori,

Well, for goodness sakes! Funny, it had never occurred to me that our paths would someday cross. Should have. Just didn't.

Yes, I will be in town that week. In fact, my annual Brief Summer Course in Infant Mental Health is that week: about two dozen people from around the U.S. come to study for a week about diagnosis and treatment of disorders of infant-parent attachment. The Course starts on Tuesday morning, August 21, and runs through the rest of the week. How long will you be here? I even have an inclination to ask about having you address the group, about your experiences with Jonathon and James.

In any event, while it will be a busy week, and one in which my attentions will be a little diverted by my responsibilities with the Course, I would love to meet you and whomever accompanies you on this mission.

What a dilemma about bringing/not bringing the kids. Of course, about a hundred alarms go off in my head when I even IMAGINE going across the country with several very needy and very demanding and more-than-a-little-unpredictable children. But I'm just an old fart, with a fraction of the courage you must have just to get out of bed each day. So, what do I know? Of course, you are also right about the price to be paid if Jonathon stays back, as you just learned when you went away that weekend. Impossible choice.

Michael

July 21, 2001

Michael,

We just finished a week of Vacation Bible School, and Jonathon had a great week! The first day was pretty bad, and Jonathon had consequences, due to a few tantrums. On day 2, Jonathon did much better. There were minor outbursts the rest of the week, but nothing too bad. Jonathon interacted with the other children, cooperated at game time, took pride in his crafts and was thrilled to report back to me at the end of each morning. It was amazing! A real success!

Last night, we had an end-of-VBS performance in front of all the parents and friends. (Our Vacation Bible School had 600 children, and the 2,000-seat sanctuary was filled with parents.) During our rehearsal at noon, Jonathon fell apart and cried. For the performance, Jonathon decided to give it a try, and he did great! We let him decide if he wanted to do it. We encouraged him, but let him make the decision. Rebecca promised to watch him closely the whole time, and be there for him if he needed to leave. He stood up with his group, sang his songs, danced the dances, and told us he had fun!

At bedtime, Jonathon told me he likes singing and dancing, likes his class, and was happy!

Compare that to the little boy who, just eight months ago, was in trouble in school every day. His former foster parents gave us notes from school that describe a violent, aggressive, completely uncooperative child. He felt isolated, insecure, and reacted accordingly. He was without hope. Now, he is not even remotely the same child. We have truly watched a miracle unfold, right before our eyes.

Adding Robin to the family mix has worked out well. She felt frustrated with Jonathon, at first. Then she attended therapy with us, and that changed her attitude towards him. She is very patient, but still consistent, with Jonathon. That is what it is all about when working with these children: attitude. If we can implement The Attitude, as I learned it from the book, *Building the Bonds of Attachment*, then we can endure and maybe have hope of progress with our children.

So Jonathon is clearly making huge progress, AND our adoption should be finalized in the next month or so.

Talk to you soon. In fact, I guess I will see you soon, too.
Lori

July 30, 2001

Dear Lori,

It was nice to arrive home late last night and find an installment from "The Saga of Jonathon" (or: "How Jonathon Got a Family But Didn't Really Want One But Yes He Did So Which Way Was He Going To Turn?").

I thought lots (on my vacation) about how other parents of children with characteristics similar to those of Jonathon would react to reading this tale, someday. I wondered if they would be angry, believing that such progress really only meant that Jonathon wasn't as severely disturbed as their children were/are. I wondered if they would find hope, or ideas, or support. Or would they only see, before their eyes, the emergence of their own dream (in Jonathon), only to look upon their particular child (NOT manifesting the dreams they had for him/her) and feel even more defeated? So many self-fulfilling prophesies... so much mystery, to how all this works.

Michael

July 31, 2001

Michael,

I have spent much time wondering the same thing about our writings. Would they help anyone, or would they just hurt because we happened to have a good deal of progress that may not have been experienced in some of the families that would read our writings?

Here are my thoughts: Early in my time with Jonathon I read the "Katy" book (*Building the Bonds of Attachment*, by Daniel Hughes). The fact that they had some very interesting episodes gave me hope and a renewed sense of humor about the whole thing. At least I knew that some of the bad that we were experiencing was "normal", and that I could expect even more. When I got to the point where they made a decision to adopt, I had mixed feelings. I really wanted to get to that point myself, and was not sure if we would. Paul was emphatically stating that there was NO hope of us arriving at that decision in unity. He was pretty frustrated, and rightfully so. But we both read the book, and gained some insight from it. It helped us to develop "The Attitude" and move forward, in spite of the frustrations. I think reading that book helped us get where we are now. If I had not read the book, our chances for success would have been less. I really believe that it took EVERY BIT of help that we received to get where we are now. It took YOU, and JON, and KATY (in the book), and SIOBHAN, and LINDSAY, and our church friends, our families, our other children, our own stubborn natures, clearly our faith in God, and our crazy sense of humor. It took good social workers, and good neighbors. A ton of reading. Even more praying. Gut- wrenching talks. Crying. Feelings of complete despair. Hope. More despair. Defeat. The ability to pick up, brush off, and open ourselves to even more hurt. And then small successes, that built upon themselves to a point where the hope outweighed the fear and despair. And at the core of it all, an incredibly sweet boy who started to emerge and show himself as someone who did want to be saved, and who was impossible to not love.

Jon has expressed interest in having other parents in his practice read what we have written, and believes that it would have a positive impact on some.

We have made some progress here towards our community. We are applying for non-profit status, and have located two parcels of land that we would love to use. We are putting together proposed time-lines, and will move forward with hope. It is the children like Jonathon that need this community. I cannot help many of them individually, but with this plan we can duplicate our efforts and reach many more. I know that that is Brenda's dream [Brenda Krause Eheart, founder of Hope] to replicate the efforts and reach the masses.

Lori

August 2, 2001

Dear Lori,

Jonathon was "…impossible not to love"? I don't think so, Lori. This statement identifies, I think, a critical juncture in your decision-making about adopting him, and, perhaps, in the whole matter of what separates your experience from that of many others. There was, indeed, something about Jonathon that grabbed you and would not let go. But that is as much about YOU as it is about Jonathon. At the risk of offending you (a risk we easily take with each other), he was NOT impossible not to love. It was possible for someone to be enraged with him, perhaps even to hate him, to objectify him, to let him go, to find his behavior purposeful/willful, to engage him in a duel as if he were actually a co-equal (and not a desperate little child fighting for his life).

So you got grabbed because:

A. You were/are grabbable?
B. You have some strange process for re-imaging a child, re-framing his behavior, having etiology play a part in how you conceptualize who a child is/why he is doing what he is doing EVERY DAY?
C. You are able to not take personally things which are, indeed, not actually about you?
D. You were called?

Don't ever imagine, however, that Jonathon was impossible not to love. He may have been impossible for YOU not to love, but that's a different matter (and one worth understanding more about). I can tell you from experience: Jonathon was an imminently rejectable child. This is something Jonathon knew (knows?). Perhaps his learning something different than this early Life Commandment is at the core of his responding to you and your life. Perhaps it is at the core of his recovery.

Michael

August 3, 2001

Dear Michael,

You MAY have a point. I will have to consider what you said. Jonathon WAS rather difficult, and some people in his past DID find him unmanageable. But he has eyes that plead his case, and a soul that cries out for love and justice and security. He gives the best hugs, but that is something that has emerged recently. In the beginning, none of those things caught my attention. His big brown eyes were full of anger, and seemed to look right through us. His soul seemed unreachable. He hit and hurt with his arms, rather than giving the hugs we are starting to enjoy. What grabbed us, in the beginning, was how pitiful his whole experience of life seemed to be. He was caught in such a vicious cycle of disruption and dysfunction, and it had to stop. Someone had to help it stop. Somehow, he ended up in our home. And somehow, it seemed only right for us to be the ones to try to stop the hurt.

What made us do it? I truly think that we did it because we were given the resources TO do it. We feel called to help hurt children, and a hurt child was plopped into our laps. Then, by "coincidence", we were given everything we needed to move forward. Every time we felt we had come to the end of the road, and knew that we were done, a breath of fresh air came our way. Sometimes it was an email full of insight from you. Sometimes it was just what we needed in therapy with Jon. Books would give us an edge that arrived not a moment too soon. A word of encouragement from a friend would be spoken seconds before we felt ready to announce to the world that this was not a match made in heaven.

But that is the bottom line, isn't it? It WAS a match made in heaven. God gave us this son, and He made the little hooks in our hearts that Jonathon was able to grab. The resources did not come to us by coincidence at all. Sure, we had to be willing to use them. We had to do some work, and the work is just beginning. But we had something to work with. It gave us hope to move forward, and the more we moved, the more hope we had, and a new cycle began—a cycle that cannot be broken, because this is what life is supposed to be. Hope, love, and security for a vulnerable and hurting child.

All of which is to say that you are right, of course. It was possible to not love Jonathon. It was not possible, however, for ME to not love Jonathon.

Lori

August 4, 2001

Dear Lori,

Yes, but what made you *breathe* that "...breath of fresh air that came your way"?! I have seen such breaths waft through the lives of many parents, and have watched as the air moved on past them (*not* through them) and on out the door. They didn't hear the insight, they didn't feel the support, they didn't see the hope, they didn't feel the pull to try (earnestly) one more thing, one more time.

Sorry to keep pushing on this (and pulling on *you*, I guess) but this seems *such* a critical matter: What, after all is said and done, separates a story like yours (plural "yours") from that of so many others that ended in disruption, or abuse and then disruption, in promised and then broken adoption, in mutual withdrawal and barely-concealed rage (on the part of the parent *and* the child)? *Why* does it seem a matter of faith? (I know *many* Christian foster parents. I really do see that there is a connection between faith and perseverance, between faith and a capacity to re-image a child. But I also know many who have given up in defeat.) Why was Paul—perhaps the standard-bearer for reality in your family—able to both see the risks and trust you about the possibilities? Why were you available for the support that came your way (instead of being so exhausted that you felt—or actually became—cut off from support, or deaf to its call)?

"What, after all is said and done, separates a story like yours from that of so many others that ended in disruption, or abuse?"
-Michael

139

And why do *you* (plural, again) know so much about hurt, that you see it, behind the irritating/embarrassing/outrageous/frightening behavior of a child? Did you—or your grandmother before you, or an uncle some generations back—have some special experience with hurt, one that prepared you to see it when it was in front of you, and not mistake it for naughtiness, or even evil?

Michael

August 5, 2001

Michael,

What did make us breathe that breath of fresh air? I don't know, exactly. Paul and I *think* the answer lies in several areas. We are experienced parents, and we know what it looks like to make progress with a child. Therefore, we also know when progress is not happening. Nothing we did with Jonathon, those first weeks, was anything close to "good" or "progress". We knew we had to try something different. That made us open to listen to ideas. Our ages and experience gave us a distinct advantage.

Having said that, I do know people who have a great deal of experience, and therefore think that they know everything. They would be unwilling to even consider doing anything different, and would just expect the child to conform and learn the way the other children had done. So maybe another part of the answer is flexibility. We have had to learn a lot about that during our years. We have had trauma and death and babies and grandfathers and many moves to keep us on our toes. We have children with special needs, teaching us to be flexible with expectations and dreams, and to treasure each person for who they are.

Patience must surely play a part. I have been married to Paul for 21 years, and you should hear his jokes! That says a lot for my patience. Certainly I have *never* done anything to try Paul's patience. These are just some ideas.

What hurt have we experienced that causes us to understand hurt when we see it? Certainly we saw a lot ten years ago when we experienced the loss of our little girl to leukemia. We lived through her hurt, and the hurt of our children when she died, and our own hurt (and anger at God) when the miracle we were waiting for did not happen. Maybe that helped to prepare us. Paul was just three months old when his mom died in a car accident. He grew up wishing for her, and his hurt was intense, at times. He felt misunderstood, and longed for the feeling of unconditional love. That love may have been offered to him, but he did not recognize it, if it was. As I write this, I realize that what I am sharing were intense losses. Certainly those must have helped us to identify with Jonathon and his many losses, and, therefore, see his hurt and find it in our hearts to endure the behavior that this hurt created.

Lori

August 6, 2001

Dear Lori,

I fear that if potential adoptive families did come face to face with what it would mean to the child if it all failed, they would all remain foster families, dedicated and determined to keep their connections with children inside the "fostering" parameters: loving the child the best way they can, knowing always that he/she is moving on (only a question of "when", not "if").

Actually, I suspect that most potential adoptive families DO know, at some level, what it means to a child to be refused. Powerful defenses must be erected in order for families to make decisions that consider other priorities of equal importance to the priority of the needy child. I understand making such a decision, and I understand the defenses needed to pull it off. My search is for what makes some families be virtually unable to do anything *other* than look past the child's behavior, and the incredible inconvenience of it all, see what the child needs, hold on long enough that the child *also* remembers what he needs and allows himself to receive it, accept support when it is offered, keep trying when any sane person would see that all is surely lost.

Michael

August 6, 2001

Dear Michael,

Jonathon and I had a great emotional connection tonight as I read "Are You My Mother?" to him (for the gazillionth time). We used a duck puppet as the baby bird, and other stuffed animals as the non-mother figures. At the end of the story, I said, "Jonathon, once a little boy came to my house and said, 'Are you my mother?', and I said, 'Yes, I am your mother.' And now I am his mother forever. That little boy is you, Jonathon." Jonathon grinned ear-to-ear and said "Yes, that's right. Mom." Then he gave me a big hug, and we cuddled for a long time. It was wonderful.

Lori

August 11, 2001

Michael,

Things here are a bit crazy, at the moment. The good news is that Jonathon's adoption may be finalized on September 4. The judge has some questions about the birth father that have not been resolved, so there is some risk. I do not think it will mean anything except a possible delay. We want the permanence to be legal as soon as possible. Jonathon deserves that.

Jonathon and James "helped" with our neighbor's move today. Jonathon was very proud of himself for being a helper. The neighbors are just moving four doors down, but Jonathon is very concerned that they will not be around anymore. I think he needed to be part of the process so that he could see where his friend's new room is. He was curious to explore the new house, but only while keeping me close to him.

Paul is going to be able to take time off while I am away, in Illinois. I think that Jonathon will handle this separation better than the last. He seems much more sure of his place in the family, and has grown and changed so much. I hope I am right.

See you soon,
Lori

August 12, 2001

Michael,

You mentioned in an email that perhaps "nothing is easy in a family like mine", or something to that effect. I know exactly what you are trying to say, but I just want to add something. You are right that planning things is not easy, as nothing goes as planned anyway. But some things *are* easy. It is easy to find someone to give me a hug, anytime of the day or night. (Someone is *always* awake and willing to spend time with mom. For example: Jonathon was still awake at 3AM last night, too keyed-up to fall asleep.) It is easy to find something to laugh about. (Something is *always* happening that can be construed as amusing. It is not always great behavior, but it *is* amusing. For example: How many moms can say that their son has urinated on a window of a pretty nice establishment in a nice part of town? Once recovering from the horror of it all, it is easy to be amused. Jonathon can never know that, of course.) Some people may thrive on a family that is stable, a family that walks a calm course down the middle of the road. But that could get boring, and I am *never* bored as I try to keep up with my children. There is always plenty to do, and someone that really needs me. Therefore, it is *easy* to find something to do. So, as you can see, some things *are* easy in a family like mine. It is all a matter of perspective.

That is not to say, of course, that I am not working towards the day when things are a bit more boring. I do want each of my children to find their course, and then walk it. The first few are firmly on their ways. I imagine, however, that by the time we get these six stable and comfortable, there will be another and we will begin the craziness again.

Lori

Dear Lori,

Have I ever mentioned that you are a little weird?

Once again, I am wondering: Why do you find humor in things that would evoke a beating out of another parent? You talk as if these things are inherently amusing, but it really IS a matter of perspective, isn't it? You can treat this as a rhetorical question, of course, but: HOW DO YOU COME TO HAVE THIS PARTICULAR PERSPECTIVE?!

Michael

August 13, 2001

Dear Michael,

Weird? Me? Could that also be something that is a matter of perspective? Hmmm...

Your question is a good one. Why do I find humor in some of the things that I do? I think I learned long ago that people who take things too seriously fail to have fun when the going gets tough. That just leads to ulcers and the like. It does not seem very beneficial. I do take things seriously, and see the need to do so. But I try to counter that with enough flexibility and humor that life remains fun. It is a balancing act.

Paul's grandfather used to live with us. He was 95, and had dementia. He had lucid moments, but not often. At the time, I had a home-based business selling baskets and pottery. At night I would go out and do shows, and come back with fewer baskets, and more money. Well, in Grandpa's day, a respectable woman did not go out at night, much less come back with money! One night I arrived home, and there were Paul and Grandpa, sitting on the sofa with their arms crossed, waiting for me. Paul announced (with a grin on his face): "Grandpa has something to say to you." Grandpa nodded and said: "Yep. I have you figured out. You are a prostitute!"

It all made perfect sense to Grandpa, who no longer had any idea who we were anyway. What was I to do—get upset, or try to convince Grandpa that he was wrong? I just laughed, and Paul laughed, and then Grandpa laughed. He had no idea why we were all laughing, now that he had caught on to my dirty secret, but he laughed with us anyway. It was a terribly sad moment, because it showed us how far gone Grandpa's mind was. It was a frustrating moment, because we were constantly dealing with the issues of raising the shell of the man that Grandpa once was. It was an embarrassing moment, to think that Grandpa could even think such a thing about me. But mostly, it was a moment in which we could all share a laugh; what else was there to do, really? The laughter fought off the tension, and the moment was soon forgotten by Grandpa. It was just one of those things that we must deal with in life.

I will give your question more thought, because I do not know the answer. There was a time when I was easily frustrated, and had a horrible temper. Many broken dishes later, I discovered that I was not doing myself or my marriage any good. That was about sixteen years ago. What made things change? Prayer. Meditation on scripture. Time. God. Children. Life lessons. All of the above.

In any case, we are happy, and thrilled to be raising the crew currently under our roof. God brought this family together, and He seems to know what He is doing.

Lori

August 13, 2001

Dear Michael,

We have just returned from a wonderful day at King's Dominion, a local amusement park. Jonathon stayed close to us the whole day, and did not try to disappear even once. He had a couple of "I am not getting my way" outbursts, but, all in all, he was fun and cooperative. He rode some of the more daring rides, and had a great time. I am amazed that we can successfully take an outing like this. Six months ago, I would have thought that this would *never* be possible.

I might be just a TAD worried about leaving Jonathon (when I come to Illinois), but I know that we will get through the separation intact. I expect some repair work to be needed, but I do not think we will need a complete overhaul. It will probably compare to a fender-bender. I will take every precaution that I can think of. I will give Jonathon a calendar, and show him when I will be home. I will ask Paul to help him mark the days off. I will give Jonathon my favorite shirt to sleep with, and maybe my special doll or a teddy bear to keep for me. I will make sure that he knows that he can call me while I am away, and I am glad about that. I also think that he will accept me when I return.

I am going to do my best to keep to a "normal" routine this week, and then ask Paul to do his best to keep to that routine next week. We have some workbooks that we do in the mornings, and that sort of thing. That should help. We will see, won't we? I hope I know what I am doing!

Jonathon just came in to check on me. It is 1:00AM, and he has been in bed for hours. Jonathon just comes in here sometimes to remind me of things, every few minutes. Sometimes he has such a hard time unwinding. It seems as if the weight of the world is on his shoulders, at times. We have talked, and brushed teeth, and had our normal routine. Jonathon just needs more reassurance some nights than others.

Lori

August 13, 2001

Dear Lori,

Has videotape (of you and the family, including Jonathon) ever worked for you? Some parents find it gives the child a more concrete sense of connection during an absence. Some kids, of course, blow it off entirely; others will sit and watch every day, sometimes rewinding to look at a favorite scene over and over. A photo can work, too, tho' you must be willing to let him "disrespect" it: tear it up, shove it in his britches, ignore it, drop it somewhere, etc. (every choice representing his feeling at the moment).

If you will still be in town on Thursday, you might want to consider coming over to the house and joining the registrants for the Brief Summer Course in Infant Mental Health (whom you will have met by then, of course) for the traditional final-evening reception. It would be a good chance to meet Mary, and I am sure the registrants would love to see you again.

Michael

August 27, 2001

Dear Michael,

I arrived back home to find Paul, Patrick, James, and Jonathon at the airport with hugs and kisses. Jonathon beamed, and continued to beam all the way home.

It was so precious. Jonathon and James brought their own toy suitcases with them, so that they could practice being the ones to travel. They stood at the gate looking incredibly cute. After hugs, Jonathon looked right at me and said, "Mom, I did a lot of crying for you. I wasn't sure if you would ever come home! I was wishing I could sleep with you. I missed you, Mom!" Then he held my hand as we made our way through the airport.

The family played a board game tonight, and sat around visiting and laughing. Jonathon was very happy to be part of it all, and I am pleased with his response tonight. He gave me a tour of the house, telling me what he did in each part. He helped Dad clean the garage, played in the back yard, ate in the dining room. He just shared it all, making sure that I was caught up on the Jonathon version of current events. He did a great job of making sure his Mommy was reconnected with his life.

Have a great weekend in that little corner of paradise where you and Mary live. What an awesome location for a home, and for the work that you do. Healing cannot help but take place there!

Lori

August 27, 2001

Dear Lori,

Well, will wonders never cease! Jonathon continues to amaze, to struggle. In this chapter, he seems to be making astounding headway in incorporating the idea of mother as one who stays, even one who goes away and comes back. It's quite a leap for him.

I hope you felt warmly welcomed here, in spite of my having limited energies and time. Did you, as did I, have difficulty adjusting to the reality of a person whom you knew-but-didn't-know?

Michael

August 27, 2001

Dear Michael,

Jonathon continues to amaze us all! Last night he asked me to cuddle him in bed, where he shared again how very sad he was while Mommy was gone, and how happy he was to have me home. He talked, and talked, and talked some more. Anything he could think of. It was exhausting, and wonderful.

We are praying for no complications, and a finalized adoption on September 4.

As for the knowing-someone-without-really-knowing-them thing: It was not hard for me at all, because you are clearly *not* the real Michael. I think you must be an alien who came and took over, in his place. The real Michael is slightly built, much more "professorly", and not quite as kind as the new you. I did enjoy getting to know the "new" you, but enjoyed even more getting to know Mary, about whom I had no misconceptions.

Lori

September 6, 2001

Hello Michael,

Remember the horrible Friday I had back a few months ago? The one where everything that could go wrong, did? Well...

Jonathon is doing well, although I did just finish a holding time. He was just wound up, and could not get under control. The holding helped, and he is responding. I cannot complain.

His adoption is moving along, slowly. It looks like we are not in any jeopardy for finalization, but it has been delayed. Birth dad issues are almost resolved, but some of the home study paperwork has now expired, and needs to be redone.

Our bad week started a week ago, when my van died. We are in the process of discovering what ails it. Then half of the electricity in the house shorted, and we are trying to fix that. Then, when we had company over for dinner, the table started to fall apart. Literally. Paul and I were trying to hold up our end without anyone noticing. Real fun! And then...

Joshua and Robin sat us down on Saturday, and said those dreadful words, "We need to tell you something..."

Joshua (19) and Robin (17) will be getting married in October, and are doing their best to live up to the adult consequences that come with an adult decision they made. We love them both, and are being supportive. We are sad for them, and the lost dreams they must now face. But reality has changed and, with it, the dreams are altered. They are good kids, and will get through this time intact. They are getting counseling, and feel certain that the decision to marry is one that they want to make. Joshua can support Robin, financially, but it won't be easy. It is so hard to see our kids go through this.

Lori

September 6, 2001

Oh, Lori, I am so sorry. I know you are trying to keep a stiff upper lip about all this, frame it well and keep it in perspective and all, but *geez...* I can imagine that you and Paul are hurt, and worried.

So now some more babies need you? The one that sat in that room inside Robin, while they told you, and these two children-who-suddenly-ended-childhood-and-have-to-pretend-to-become-parents. They aren't, of course. My wish across these many state lines is that Robin and Joshua find the support they need to calm their hearts and their chemistries, so they can communicate welcome to this baby, so they can tell this baby not that he wrecked their lives and is somehow responsible for *them,* now, but that he/she is safe and can lie quietly and take in all they have to give. This baby does not need to hide in shame, does not need to try to disappear to reduce Robin's and Joshua's burden. The three of them will need so much prayer.

I know that this sort of thing can sometimes create a particular strain between a boy like Joshua and his father, who may be awfully disappointed. I hope they can find their way through to manly support and love.

And I wish for you and Paul complete relief from second-guessing, trying to imagine what you could have done differently, taking on what is not yours. Perhaps all your experience with kids in need, where you had to give up any pretense that you could make things come out *any* particular way, will help you, here.

And why, *why*, did your van pick this week to die, or your table to droop, or your house to fizzle. Is God in a *really* bad mood, or does God think this is *funny*?! What symbolism in my mental picture of you and Paul attempting to hold up the table, with joint effort, so that maybe no one would notice, maybe everything wouldn't collapse (after all), maybe people wouldn't see how things were sagging in the Thomas house. Whew...

My thoughts and prayers are with all of you, including the newest member, who is very much there for all that is happening, right now, tonight.

Michael

September 6, 2001

Dear Michael,

Did you know that little boys cannot fly? Jonathon just told me so. Yesterday we were at a homeschool picnic with our friends, and Jonathon was swinging with some other boys. He saw them jumping out in mid-air, and thought it looked fun. He was really up there when he decided to let go. He thought he was flying, and really enjoyed it. Until the landing. Flat on his face. He is not too much the worse for it all, and he wears the scab on his forehead proudly. He was trying to fly.

I laughed as I got your mental picture of us and the table. We have had to remove one of the leaves of the table and tighten a few things, and the table is once again strong enough. Not perfect, but it works. That is life, isn't it? We try to remove that which does not work, strengthen that which does, and go on.

I am very aware of the presence of little Zachary/Heidi in our lives. Joshua and Robin will be loving parents, even if they are a bit young. They do have the advantage of lots of experience, including with our wonderful Jonathon.

All in all, things could be better, but they could also be much worse. They could not, however, be much more exciting. Never a dull moment.

I watched Jonathon sitting with Paul, tonight: laughing and enjoying some moments together, and I noticed how natural they look together. They were both relaxed, and they just fit. They were clearly father and son. It was very nice.

That is all, for now.
Lori

September 6, 2001

Dear Lori,

You made me recall the day my middle son, Ben (now studying to become a school psychologist) decided to fly. He used a little umbrella, and sailed off the top of a much-too-tall structure at the park. He broke a part of his foot that could not be set, but I also think it broke his heart that it did not work. It seems only a short time ago, and now his body is so big. I love it that he has retained some of that same wonder, and a little naiveté.

What a strange time for your family, as you wait, and watch, as a few more things climb up on your plate, even as you continue waiting.

Michael

September 7, 2001

Dear Michael,

I look forward to the day when I can recount the flying story, and state that it was Jonathon, my sixth child, who gave it a try. And that Jonathon is now studying to be a school psychologist, or a pediatrician, or some other grand ambition. He will look quite striking in a white lab coat, with his very tall and dark body. He will be properly compassionate, considering his own hurts as he frames his understanding of life, and his fellow man, and relationships. He will have had the wonderful connections with his nuclear family from which to reach out and grow. What a story he will have to share with others.

I cannot even begin to describe the level of love that has grown in my heart for my little Jonathon. He is a wonderful person, with much to share. I hope and pray that we can completely reach him. He has opened up some of himself, but still keeps quite a bit in reserve. I am in awe of the parts that he has shared. If I were a child with his history, I do not think I would be nearly as good at the work of healing. But Jonathon is working hard, and it is paying off.

Jonathon and James are going to be co-ringbearers in the Joshua and Robin wedding! Do you think they have a chance of actually getting their rings? Should be quite a sight! Maggie is the flower girl. Rebecca is a bridesmaid. Patrick is the best man, and Robin's sister is the maid of honor.

The baby (my grandchild) just needs to stay where she is, and grow, and be a baby.

Time to get my little flying boy going on his school work!

Lori

September 8, 2001

Michael,

Jonathon continues to struggle with the security of believing that he is our son, forever. This is a hard time for the little guy, but we will just keep working with him. We are spending lots of time, as a family, playing board games and, in general, making sure all the kids are feeling bonded and protected and free to share feelings and fears.

Hope all is well with you,
Lori

September 12, 2001

Dear Michael,

What a tragedy our nation faced yesterday, and will continue to experience for a long time to come. I cannot believe that it happened here, in our land. It does not seem real; at the same time, it is clearly all too real.

How do we heal from such a day? Do we rally together, renew our patriotism, and stand proudly against our foes? I hope so. At the same time we mourn the lives lost, and we try to comfort those who paid the highest cost with the loss of a loved one.

On Monday evening (9-10-01), before all of this happened, we had a fire in the kitchen. It was relatively minor. We were able to put it out with fire extinguishers before it spread beyond the stove and one cabinet. The cleanup necessary after that one little fire is incredible. I am scrubbing walls and ceilings on the whole first floor. I will need to repair the cabinets, and then paint all of them. I will also need to paint the walls and ceiling in the kitchen, and pull down the destroyed wallpaper borders. The vent over the stove, and the stove, itself, need to be replaced, along with a couple of pots and pans that were on the stove, at the time.

If a small fire can cause that much destruction, and the necessary repairs will take days, how does a city recover from what happened there (in New York)? It is beyond my imagination.

So our country is in shock this morning, my home is in disarray, and my youngest son is having a tough time. It actually started four days ago. Clearly, he is responding to the stress he feels in our home (in relation to the upcoming wedding, etc.), to the change in routine (the beginning of the school year), and, maybe, to the pending adoption. In addition, we are at the eight-month point with Jonathon, which is about the time that his last two placements began to disrupt. Jonathon's behavior is pretty close to that of last January, when he first arrived in our home. We are cutting out all extra activities, and spending a lot of time closely supervised, and at home. More holding time (in general, just for the fun of it, as well as in response to his behaviors), and lots of together time.

The good news behind all of this: We are a strong family, with good support, so we will survive our personally difficult times. And we are a strong country, so we will overcome these attacks against us and come out even stronger, in the end.

Life as we know it has halted in Northern Virginia. Any place where large groups might congregate is closed. Schools, malls, many business buildings: all are shut down, for now.

Our prayers are with those still trapped, and the rescuers who are attempting to reach them. May this be a day of rejoicing, as many are pulled free from the ruins, alive and well.

We send best wishes to you and your precious family.
Lori

October 31, 2001

Dear Michael,

It's amazing how a tragedy can get life into perspective. The events of 9-11 did, indeed, change our country—and, in turn, my own perspective of what is important, and what did not really matter.

Before 9-11, I was growing weary. We had made the decision to adopt Jonathon, but the process took longer to complete than expected. In the meantime, Jonathon continued to show us enough negative behaviors that we grew concerned about our decision.

On the morning of September 11, 2001, I was teaching in our home-school co-op. One of my friends stuck her head in the door about 9:30 or so, and asked me to step into the hall. Her news made my head spin. How could an airplane hit such a huge building? How could such an accident happen? As the day went on, and it became clear that this was an intentional act of terrorism, my motherly instincts took over. I gathered my children from their respective locations and kept then all in my line of vision at home. It seemed logical to bake something.

My letters to you ceased for several weeks. I was no longer as concerned about behaviors or about therapy. I just wanted to know where my children were at all times, and knew I would do anything to protect them.

This nurturing attitude could not have come at a better time for Jonathon. With the decision to adopt behind us, and so much progress already happening, it was good to take a few weeks to just hang out and be together. We did not stop our holding therapy at home, or let him get away with his constant "crazy lying" or destructiveness, but we did relax just a bit, and try to enjoy every moment we had together as a family.

Some of our friends lost loved ones on September 11. One of our church members was killed at the Pentagon. For weeks, the Washington, D.C. area remained wary. We mourned, as people across our nation and all around the world also mourned.

Life has begun to return to its normal patterns, but our thankfulness for each other has remained heightened.

Lori

November 1, 2001

Michael,

I figured it was about time to send you an update about Jonathon, and his progress! It has been a crazy month around here but, for once, Jonathon was not at the center of the storm.

Joshua and Robin's wedding went well, and Jonathon and James were PERFECT ring-bearers. They walked down that aisle like pros, and were both as cute as can be.

Jonathon is really seeming very happy, and his confidence level increases daily. Right now I would describe him as an active (okay, *very* active), happy, strong-willed child. That is a lot better than any description I would have given in past months. Jon has suggested we cut our therapy down to once a month and see how it goes. I agree that we are okay to do that at this time. An exciting thought.

Paul is away at a retreat this weekend, and Jonathon is unsettled by his absence. Jonathon finally got to sleep last night about 1AM, and then I found that he had crawled into bed with me about 3AM. He often is a challenge at bedtime (often as in "almost always" and "If there was ever a night that he was not a challenge, I do not seem to be able to recall it") but lately has been able to calm down within an hour. Last night, and so far tonight, the one-hour settle-down period does not seem to be in effect. I can understand why, though, so I will be firmly patient until sleep arrives.

Jonathon has joined the children's choir at church, and they will be singing tomorrow morning. Another exciting development for my little boy.

We are due to have our adoption finalized on 4 November, and hope for no more delays. There will be a big party at the Thomas house planned for later in November, in celebration of the finalization! (You and Mary do not happen to want to make a trip to Virginia, do you?)

Hope all is well with the Trout Family in Illinois.
Lori

November 2, 2001

Dear Lori,

There is such a new tone to your communication, probably reflecting the [relative] peace in your house? What an unusual thing, for a child with RAD, that he actually knew what he needed clearly enough to climb into bed with you at 3AM. This, alone, tells me how much progress he has made in your family, and in therapy. It also raises the hope that his past includes a period when he received—perhaps not consistently, but from time to time—some good-enough mothering. He seems to be falling back on an old knowledge.

It would be wonderful to be at the shindig celebrating the adoption finalization. A thought did go through my mind about what sort of melt-down might match the occasion for Jonathon, but perhaps I am just too cautious...

Very good to hear from you again.
Michael

November 7, 2001

Dear Michael,

I just received a call from our social worker, and we might have a sig-nature for finalization late this week! In Virginia, the family does not go to court. The judge, in the privacy of his chambers, signs a paper and lets you know that "It Is Finished".

I laughed when you stated that we might expect a meltdown, and then commented on the fact that maybe you are just too cautious. Cautious cannot be an apt description for you, as cautious people do not knowingly add children with RAD to their homes. "Cautious" is, in my mind, a bad word. There is not much adventure in it. "Throw caution to the wind" is almost equivalent to "carpe diem". There is never a point in doing something that is just plain stupid, like running in front of a truck just for the fun of it. But there is a point in taking risks, if there is something worthwhile at stake. The life of a child, for instance. I would run in front of a truck to get a child to safety. All that is to say that I do not see you as cautious. Wise, yes. Experienced, of course. But you take risks every day in your work, and that allows you to reach into souls that others may have thought were not reachable.

The tone of our lives here in Virginia has changed quite a bit. Jonathon is clearly continuing to fight *for* emotional health, and he is winning. He wants to be happy, I think. That gives us a *huge* advantage over so many parents who are struggling with children that have given up completely. Looking back over the past ten months, I do not think that Jonathon had given up all hope. Clearly, someone—at some point—had given him reason to believe that he could be loved. I know that one of his foster families truly cared for him and treated him as a precious child. That time with them, sandwiched between other placements where there may have been neglect and abuse, had an impact. Attachment Disorder had been suggested before that placement, and Jonathon displayed lots of his challenges while with them, but he did see love there. Certainly that helped him survive the hatred that he seemed to feel and experience in his next placement. I am very thankful for any positive experiences that he had prior to our home. It certainly made our job possible.

As I write this, I hear Jonathon having a difficult time downstairs, but Rebecca seems to have it under control. Sounds like maybe she is holding him, and they are having a talk about the importance of obeying the rules. I do not hear the words "blood" or "call 9-1-1", so I will let Rebecca handle it.

We have the best home school co-op, and I am thankful for the patience of the other moms in our group. Jonathon is starting to participate more and more. There have been a few problems. Last week he lied to the teacher about eating his sandwich, when he had actually thrown it in the bushes. This week he stole another boy's balloon, and lied to me about it. It clearly said "Patrick" on it, but Jonathon claimed he just spelled his name differently today. He looked at me as if he was fully aware that he had been caught, but showed no emotion. Maybe we have a ways to go with the crazy-lying stuff. We will get there.

I have this funny thought going through my head. Jonathon continues to break things. It is usually not intentional. Just a result of disobedience. Who would expect a hard ball, thrown in the living room, to smash into the Korean vase that mom had decided was relatively safe on the coffee table? Anyway, the thought: I am tempted to take the pieces of broken things, and store them for future use. I see potential for a piece of art. Some kind of beautiful sculpture, or mosaic. Tiny pieces of broken things, made into something new and beautiful. It would symbolize the lives of these broken children. The children, like the broken vases, are never the same as they would have been. They are beautiful, and they are wonderful. But they are not the same children as they would have been if they had not been broken by abuse and neglect. The trick is to keep the broken pieces without becoming bitter about the loss of the original item. Just as the trick with children is to help them recover from their pasts without allowing bitterness to fill them. It is one thing to acknowledge that things were not good, at some point. It is quite another to become bitter because of the not-good times.

During the few minutes that I have been typing, I have had three interruptions. One was a phone call. One was a knock at the door. As I answered the door, Jonathon ran outside and climbed up onto our friend's truck. Screamed at the top of his lungs. Came down fairly easily, but then climbed up a second time. Consequences were to come inside, and not be allowed out again today. (It is almost dark anyway.) Consequences if he does it again will be to miss a party we are going to tomorrow. The third interruption was Jonathon, announcing that he no longer loves me. Oh, well. Five minutes ago, he was going to love me forever. Now, it is over. Easy come, easy go. I let him know that I love him forever.

So, throwing caution to the wind, we are planning our adoption finalization party.

Lori

November 8, 2001

Dear Lori,

So many smiles come from reading your letters…

Keeping the broken pieces seems chock full of meaning, doesn't it? I keep thinking of the notion that the sculpture, "Michelangelo" was already inside the block of marble, waiting to come out. What should be our working model, with children like Jonathon? That a precious, once-loved child is in there, all the while—through all the crazy lying, the violence, the affective spin-arounds, the hateful statements—waiting to come out? Or do we see ourselves as armed with glue, putting together pieces that life and ugly experience have broken apart? What about the fact that we don't actually *know* what is inside (if anything, we must wonder, some days!), much less whether there is some kind of essential goodness, or an essential evil that we must somehow re-shape, re-form?

I suppose, it could be fun demonstrating what can be made of broken pieces. I have always known there is a good reason that we have "Humpty Dumpty" as a child's nursery rhyme: it displays a dilemma, or solves a problem, from the perspective of a little child.

A patient recently gifted me with a "shard box", from China, and explained that such things (a gorgeous little copper box with a curved painted-china lid) are made with the broken pieces of various cultural icons (some valuable, some mundane) that were destroyed in China during the Cultural Revolution. I gather that they were seen, by the government, as symbolizing the wealth and class-consciousness of China before communism, before the revolution. But the pieces were sometimes kept, and are now being turned into keepsake containers. My patient thought it was a fitting symbol of the work we had done, discovering and treasuring old and broken pieces, and trying to fit them together, again—not as they were, but in new forms.

Mary and I take every opportunity, these days, to look back just a year ago, and count our blessings for the astounding progress Jeremy has made. I gave him some consequences today for talking disrespectfully to his mother, whereupon both she and I looked back in amazement that we would ever be thinking about something so minor, when his disrespect *used* to express itself in rages and screaming and kicking and flailing his whole body at her (not merely a word or tone of voice)! The whole family is having to adjust, by the way, to his no longer taking up all the space, his no longer "sucking all the air out of the room". It changes the dynamic of the family when Jeremy is not doing his part anymore to fulfill the role of permanently and reliably disabled little brother, who could be counted on to be dopey and make his parents crazy.

I'm picturing the judge doing his/her thing, alone, in chambers. Such an enormous thing it is. Seems as tho' someone ought to be watching...

Michael

December 27, 2001

Dear Michael,

We have just celebrated a wonderfully peaceful Christmas, and know that we have so much to be thankful for this year! I thought it appropriate to share some of it with you.

We kept Christmas simple, with just our family. The preparations were hectic, as they tend to be, but we kept the outside activities to a minimum this year. We all went to see Santa as a family, and Jonathon reminded Saint Nick that he has a new home and family. He did not want Santa to get confused and take his gifts to the wrong house. We all assured Jonathon that there was no problem, and that all involved parties are very much in tune with the fact that Jonathon is a Thomas, now. And forever.

On Christmas eve we had a live nativity at church. Jonathon was interested in baby Jesus, and the story of His birth. James was wondering why the donkey does not have udders like the cow.

We have lots of traditions around this special day, and Jonathon was quite attentive to them. We have a Christmas pyramid from Germany—the kind with candles, and the figures that rotate. Jonathon loves that, and we burn it at dinner each night. He also enjoyed cutting down a tree, baking cookies, eating cookies, and decorating the house. We went out looking at Christmas lights, caroling, and watched as Rebecca and her youth group performed with their puppets—lots of family memories in the making. Every tradition we have we really emphasized this year, so that the memories include Jonathon. I wanted him to know that all of these traditions are *his*.

Christmas day we had just the nine of us, and it was perfect.

We know that we are blessed beyond measure. For Jonathon to be this tuned in to this family, and to feel as comfortable as he seems to, is such a joy to us.

Jonathon just came to me, and says he wants me to get a cup of coffee and come visit with him. I will finish this note later...

I'm back. Our coffee time was nice. Jonathon wanted to share some of his thoughts with me. Said he had some bad dreams, but he does not remember them. Just wanted to talk.

Jonathon's adoption is not yet finalized, and it is driving me crazy. We don't think there is any particular problem, just delays with the holidays and all of that. Nevertheless, I will be much happier when those final papers are in my hands with the appropriate signatures on them.

Our best wishes to you and your family during this wonderful season. We are thankful for the impact that you have had on our family, which is part of the reason that we have so much to celebrate this year!

Lori and crew

December 28, 2001

Dear Lori,

I was just about to sit down and write a Christmas message to you, when yours arrived. As usual, your words evoke visual images galore, and I'm grateful for that (as it helps me feel much more connected to Jonathon's life there).

I'm sure this must be a sentimental time for you and Paul, as thoughts of where you all were one year ago come flooding over you. So much has been settled, and has been able to settle, since then. So many barriers to overcome; so many behaviors to contend with, to watch unfold, and to try to respond to. So many reactions from the rest of your family members (obvious and visible, and subtle and less visible) to notice and appreciate. Roller coasters of feeling that you must all have tried to flatten out, as you really couldn't live life and ride to those highs and lows everyday (at least without getting ill!). I know that you say there was really never a decision to make: Jonathon was yours; it would just take a while for the rest of the world to get up to speed, and join you in that realization. But I also know that there was a great deal going on inside both you and Paul, as you struggled to understand what you were capable of, what Jonathon was capable of, and what was best for all.

I am honored to have been able to go along for some of the ride. Certainly I learned more than I taught, and gained more than I gave. I hope we don't lose contact. My very best to you all.

Michael

chapter VI.

Epilogue: Moving On

*"I guess doggies' whiskers don't
catch on fire!" (Jonathon)*

January 16, 2002

Dear Michael,

Jonathon Thomas is now a legal name. His adoption is finalized!

As I read the final adoption decree, I was shocked at the level of emotion that rose up in me. It was just a piece of paper, declaring something that I already knew to be true. But that one little paper, with one little signature, means the world to me. It makes legal the relationship between me and my son, and cements that bond forever. It is a precious paper, and I cried like a baby when I finally received it. Jonathon is my son!

Jonathon was happy that "the paper from the judge" arrived in the mail, and when I showed it to him he gave me a big hug. Then he and Maggie disappeared into his room to talk about something. Being the good mom that I am, I eavesdropped. I stood there, ear to door, listening to their conversation. Maggie asked, "Jonathon, do you know that I was adopted, too?" Jonathon's reply was interesting. "Does that mean you lived with G. [a former foster mother], too?" "No," Maggie answered. "I lived in Korea, in an orphanage. But when Mom and Dad adopted me, I became part of this family. Now this is my forever family, just like it is yours. That means I never have to leave. You never have to leave, either." Jonathon screamed, "You mean I *really* never have to go back to G's?" He ran from the room, and right into me, since I was still eavesdropping outside the door. He grabbed me, and held tight. "Mom, I never have to go back to G's! Isn't that great?"

The hold that this one foster family has had over Jonathon, and the concern that has clearly remained deep inside him, makes me so sad for him. On the other hand, the response to our finalization was wonderful. I am thrilled and relieved to know that our adoption process is finished. This is a child who needs to know that he can stay in one place and work on life with some security. With a family that adores him.

So, we are all happy as can be, and starting this New Year off just the way we wanted!

Just wanted to share our joy with you,

Lori

January 17, 2002

Dear Lori,

It's amazing, isn't it, that what we offer to children in child welfare (protective services, adoption services, foster care) sometimes hurts them as much as whatever trauma, abuse, or neglect we were saving them from in the first place? Knocks me out that he talks so much about the experience with the one foster family. Undoubtedly, there is some transference; he may be able to conceptualize, to make concrete and conscious, his experience there, more than he can his earliest experiences with his mother. He may also be doing some serious splitting, as a defensive strategy to buoy his sense of safety now, or to help him feel clearer about his own feelings. Still, it is clear that, in the name of helping him, he must have gotten hurt again in that home.

Thanks for including me in this moment. I am thrilled for all of you. You must have been pretty impressed with Maggie's articulateness. I'm intrigued that this is not a moment of trauma for Jonathon; he seems to have been down the road (of doubt, terror about continued loss and anxiety about closeness) enough times that this court action hasn't thrown him for a loop.

I will be thinking about you all.

Michael

January 21, 2002

Dear Michael,

Yesterday and today have been reflective days for me, and I wanted to share some of my thoughts with you.

We are about to celebrate our church's 25th anniversary, and our pastor made mention of it during his sermon. While anniversaries are important, and looking back has great value, he wanted to encourage all of us to continue to look towards the future with our hopes, dreams, and goals. He said, "Dreams for the future must be bigger than memories from the past." It all brought to mind something that I have often heard quoted in the past: "Without a vision, the people perish."

The rest of the sermon was a blur to me, as I sat and considered his words, and the implications for children like Jonathon. Dreams for the future *must* be bigger than memories (of abuse or neglect, memories that are bad, memories that can be magnified in the mind for bad *or* good) from the past. So how do we create hopes and dreams in a child who has so little good in his past from which to draw? If there is no frame of reference for hope, can a child feel hope?

Clearly, the moment at hand, the present, is the place to begin. The holding therapy, the work of trying to build a sense of security: it is all about trying to build new memories and a basis from which to draw hope for the future.

Jonathon had some positive memories from his past which we could use and build upon. It made our work much easier, because he had some good to counteract the bad. What about the children who truly have no good upon which to build—or so much bad that it erases the good from their minds?

My thought pattern has been interrupted. I just learned that there was a shooting in Arlington last night, in which two women and a 6-year-old child were killed. It turns out that one of the women was one of Siobhan's former foster children (she was the social worker) and there was an 18-month-old child at the scene that is currently on her caseload. The baby was not injured (physically!), but it appears the mom was holding her at the time of the shooting. Blood all over the baby. Siobhan had to go and identify the body of the mom last night. And place the baby in a foster home. Pretty traumatic for all involved.

Another phone call today was from a mom of one of the wrestlers on Jonathon's team. They are new to the area, and are having trouble with their child, who is about Jonathon's age. She called me for advice. She wanted to know if I could help her because she is impressed with what a gentle, sweet boy Jonathon is! Her child has tantrums, and is pushing her to her limit. She is yelling a lot, losing control, and wants to know if we have ever experienced that with any of our children. I am meeting with her tomorrow morning. I plan to share some of our struggles with her, let her know how successful "The Attitude" and holding have been in dealing with Jonathon, and recommend a couple of books.

Anyway, back to the issue of building dreams for a future in our children. I just thought it interesting on this, Martin Luther King's birthday, to talk about dreams for a better tomorrow. I DO HAVE A DREAM, and in my dream I see a grown up, well-adjusted Jonathon. He is a positive member of society, and he is happy. I think he sees that dream, too, and it thrills me!

Lori

January 24, 2002

Dear Lori,

You are right, of course, that therapy often takes long, in-depth looks at the past. But one of the things I am always searching for is *The Exception*: that person or event, sometimes only briefly-known, that stands out amongst all the mess and violence and deprivations, and says to the baby, or child, in effect: "Yes, much of your life has sucked. You are probably fast on your way to deciding that all of life will be like this, that you have no defense except to stop expecting anything good to happen to you, and to everlastingly prepare yourself for loss. But, hold on. Remember me. Can you save room for this experience that we have had together, and not quite fully despair, yet?"

When I teach, I call it "The Aunt Rosie Syndrome", in honor of one of the first cases in which I learned about the phenomenon. Sometimes Aunt Rosie is, literally, a family member to whom the child escaped from time to time (when mom or dad was drunk or being abusive); or a neighbor on whose lap the toddler would sometimes find an unfamiliar comfort; or a relative who stopped over only every few months, but whom the child knew could influence mom or dad to beat less or hold more; or a person at the orphanage; or, of course, a foster parent. I don't hold any fantasies that Aunt Rosie can turn the child's life around. But I have seen, over and over, that such an exception in a child's life can come back to haunt them, in the most positive of senses, years later. I've been with children and grownups in therapy when the feeling will come back: of being held, of being looked at, of being praised, of being *seen*. It can be mighty powerful.

The whole question of how to build/create hope in a child is such a tough one. You and I have talked before about the transactional nature of development: truly negative early experiences sometimes create such shifts in the child's sense of self, in the child's expectations, that he begins to negatively influence his caregivers, and others. People pull back, withhold commitment, don't want to be around him. Self-fulfilling prophecies abound. A foster parent, or adoptive parent, or therapist who tries to stop that locomotive of self-destruction has an overwhelming job. Sometimes we get lucky, and sometimes we don't.

One of the things that came to me when I was writing my own dream about children and culture was that dreams are not just idle fantasies. Dreams, in my view, become expectations, visions of the world as it should be—*and as it's going to be, if I have anything to say about it, which I do!* I really believe this is why Dr. King had such an impact with his speech. He wasn't blowing smoke. He actually expected that the things he was saying could happen, and you just knew that he was not about to be stopped in his quest to make it so. He would never lose his vision, because it would inform his every act, every day.

We should continue this conversation…

Michael

January 24, 2002

Dear Michael,

What is a dream, anyway? I looked in my children's dictionary, and found very incomplete definitions. My thinking is that a dream is something that you want so badly that a plan is formed, and *nothing* can stop you from moving forward with that plan. Temporary setbacks and slow progress are not deterrents. They are just times to take a deep breath and build up the courage to move forward again.

A dream, then, is hope put into action.

I have a dream to open a community where children who have been hurt by life will have a chance to be loved, to heal, to be a member of a family that cherishes them just because they are who they are. This dream is taking form here in northern Virginia, largely because others share the dream.

Lori

April 8, 2002

Happy spring, Michael,

James just headed off for a day of school after Jonathon, James and I had a particularly great breakfast together. As we chatted, Jonathon started telling us the rules of life. It began with safety. Buckle up, sit in your seat, and wear the seatbelt across your belly, not around your neck. Then he reminded us of the crossing-the-street rules. Once he got started, he was on a roll. He talked about the rules of appropriate yelling (outside is best, and don't yell at your friends). He just kept going. Table rules. Safety rules. How-to-treat-your-dog rules. Rules that I was quite sure he did not know: Don't play in a car without a grownup there. Rub Gidget's head and she will love you.

Jonathon has recently celebrated his one-year anniversary in the Thomas family (January 19), his sixth birthday (March 30), and his first big drama production. He had a few lines as part of a crowd scene in our homeschool's production of "Hello Dolly". It was a grand production, with an audience of 250 people, and Jonathon handled his role splendidly.

Jonathon just now climbed up on my lap, and is singing, "Twinkle, Twinkle Little Star, How I Wish I could go to Disney World". In real life, he will be flying to California with me and James on April 19th. We will go to see Joshua and Robin and baby Heidi, who was due to be born on March 30, but has not chosen to make her debut just yet. While in California, I plan to take the boys to Disneyland. We will have a chance to love the new grandbaby, while we're at it. Jonathon will be an uncle!

Jonathon is, at this point, a lot of fun and a huge challenge. There are so many issues that we are still dealing with, and some weeks I feel like all I do is hold Jonathon, and try to see the light of day. But those weeks are becoming the exception, rather than the rule. Routinely, Jonathon is difficult and a handful. But he is making such wonderful progress! His sweet side is showing up more and more.

And then we have mornings like today, when all is right with the world. Jonathon's progress has been more than I would have dreamed for, a year ago. It has been a year that I would prefer to never repeat. But, then, again, it was a year that was so very much worth living.

This is the current state of the Thomas family: happy, relatively well settled, enjoying life as it is in this moment, looking forward to the future, thankful that the past has been lived just as it was, thankful to God for all our blessings, with our six children being at the top of the blessings list. We cannot imagine life without any of them.

I just got THE CALL. Heidi is on the way!
Lori

April 8, 2002

Dear Lori,

You are very sweet to think of sending me a progress report. Hard to believe how fast the time has passed. (Easy for *me* to say, since I wasn't living *your* life!) The summary sounds exactly right: had to happen, wouldn't want to do it again, astounding progress, still an enormous challenge, can still remember why you're doing this, even when the feedback isn't always there. And, in the middle of it all, life is being lived, history is being made, memories are being laid down, principles are being absorbed…

I had a minor stroke a month ago. It has thrown our family for a loop, as you can imagine, tho' we're doing OK. Jeremy greeted me at the back door when I arrived home from the hospital with a list he had made of all the things he thought I might not be able to do, anymore, and offering his help with each one. You could have knocked me over with a feather (well, actually, you could have *anyway,* due to the unsteadiness of my gait!): a child with his history and customary self-absorption, showing empathy.

Thanks for letting me have a place in your lives.
Michael

April 8, 2002

Dear Michael,

You are in the Thomas family prayers. Full recovery, peace for your family, and all of that good stuff. I am assuming that you are doing well, since your email was vintage Michael. Sounded just like you, which I will take as a good sign.

Have you considered publishing an edited version of our correspondence? I sure would love it if your wisdom, and our collective experiences with our children, could help those that don't have you available to them the way we did.

Lori

April 11, 2002

Dear Lori,

Looks as if I get to keep my brain and my speech, my face doesn't sag, and I can still do most things. I have no feeling on the left side of my body, I wobble some, fall over occasionally (you can imagine that I try to be dignified about it!), and experience a tremor from time to time.

Indeed, I have often thought of what creative thing should be done with our letters. The fact that I so often think of things you have said or Jonathon has done, while consulting with families, makes it seem as if such a publication would have a purpose, and an audience. But I don't know.

Michael

> *"If we had been presented with the whole picture up front, Jonathon would never have entered our door. We would not have been willing. But now changed life is appearing right before our eyes."*

April 13, 2002

Dear Michael,

I was thrilled to get your email, and hear your positive attitude shining so brightly in the midst of what has to be a very difficult time. There are at least a gazillion people who are thankful that your brain was not affected, and that your speech and sense of humor are intact! The stumbling from time to time, while a problem and something that we pray goes away, makes you more human to those of us who look up to you.

Last night, I became intensely aware of the spoken word and its import and impact on those with whom we have the opportunity to speak. My spoken words were directed at Jonathon, and it was in the midst of a very sad and intense situation. Some of my children were in the back yard, burying Gimli, the recently-departed hamster. Jonathon and James did not want to be part of the funeral, and were headed upstairs to get ready for a bath. Suddenly, we heard hitting and screaming. James ran downstairs, with Jonathon right behind him, denying that he had done anything wrong. James ran to us, sobbing and saying, "Jonathon hit. Jonathon hit." There were several red marks across James' back. In the matter of a few seconds, Jonathon was able to hurt James, and shake us all up, rather significantly.

Paul tended to James, and I sat down, face-to-face with Jonathon. I was angry, and, in my mind, the words I formed were all wrong. I took a couple of deep breaths, and thought before I spoke. What I wanted to say was, "How *dare* you hurt my James! He is my son, and you can't hurt him. I love you, but I will not let you hurt my James again!" Actually, I did not want to say those words. I wanted to yell them. And then follow up with consequences. Severe consequences. That is what I wanted to do and say.

By taking the time to think, I was able to realize how wrong those words would be, when directed toward Jonathon. The first word I identified and knew I had to erase *before* it was spoken was "but". I changed it to "and", as in: "Jonathon, I love you, *and* I love James, and I will not let you hurt him. By hurting him, you showed me that I have given you too much freedom. I need to take that freedom away until I see that I can trust you to not hurt other people. That means that for one week Mommy is going to watch you very closely. You will not be allowed to be alone with James, and you will not be allowed to have friends over. Mommy will need to stay with you all the time, the way we used to do it. Then, when I see that you have remembered how to play nicely with James, I will start to give you a little bit of freedom, again".

The second word that I deleted was "my", when referring to James. Jonathon is just as much mine as James is, and I will not make him feel otherwise. Little words like "but" and "my", and they can make such a difference in a message. I am not sure if I handled the situation as well as I could have, but I do know that I handled it better that I would have if I had not thought before speaking. (I did take into account the fear and sadness associated with the death of Gimli, and addressed that matter with all of the children. I think that had a lot to do with the whole episode.)

And that is all the news from this part of the world, for now.

Lori

April 16, 2002

Dear Lori,

You've captured something that is very hard to teach (to parents)—indeed, very hard for any of us to acquire, unless the heart is ready.

Of course, communications go downhill fast all the time because the first few words contain hidden explosives: hidden to the parent (who acted on impulse, or simply didn't "catch" how meaningful and hurtful the words would be), and hidden to the child (who knows he feels very bad, but may actually not identify the hurtful word/words as the reason).

So children go blithely on, injured and reeling and furious, but not knowing why. Parents leave the encounter feeling vaguely as if the child didn't learn anything (which is probably true) and as if something didn't go right, but they are uncertain what.

But you captured all the key elements:

1. You are my son, same as you were before you clobbered your brother.
2. I still love you, same as before you clobbered your brother.
3. I will absolutely not allow you to hurt your brother (and I will not allow him or others to hurt you).
4. I take responsibility for helping you, and see that I may have not helped you by giving you too much freedom.
5. The solution to this will not be withdrawal on the part of either of us. Indeed, it will be just the opposite: you are going to need to stay near me for a while, so I can help you remember to manage those feelings inside of you.
6. While this may seem like punishment, and you may not like it, it isn't, and we're going to do it, anyway.
7. You may think I am protecting James and punishing you. I hope you come to see that I will always protect you, also: both from others, and from the mad feelings inside of you.

Now that that's all settled, there might be time (later) for wondering about the fact that somebody died. Sometimes you might get sadness mixed up with madness, and I'll bet I can help you with that, too. You may think Gimli left YOU. You may be mad at Gimli for dying. Maybe you think Daddy or I could die, if Gimli could. Let's draw a picture about it. Or, maybe you'd like to SHOW me what happened, with these toys.

Anyway, Lori, I get your point, and it's a dandy. I have seen such incidents break the back of a placement—particularly after a time of relative peace, and the presumption that "all the bad stuff is behind us". That's a particularly vulnerable time for a parent, which makes it a time when the wrong words come easily, and the right words are incredibly elusive.

My best,
Michael

May 8, 2002

Dear Michael,

Thought I would give you an update on Jonathon, and his travels to meet the relatives. It was quite a trip!

As we prepared to leave Virginia, Jonathon cuddled with Rebecca on the couch, and stated: "I wish my whole family could go. I am going to miss my family." Teary-eyed, he hugged Rebecca and let her know that he would miss her especially much.

Both boys were excited about the trip, and the airplane ride. Unfortunately, our first plane was a turbo-prop, from here to Pittsburgh. The noise was too much for James and his autism, and the bouncing was too much for Jonathon. He announced, many times, that we were going to crash. James handled his stress by closing his eyes and trying his hardest to sleep, which was not successful. He was pretty distressed. Jonathon worried aloud the complete hour. I held him, tried to distract him, and attempted to assure him that all was well with the plane—that the noises and bounces were part of the ride on this type of plane, and to be expected. He was not convinced, and became pretty vocal as we banked and prepared to land. I am sure the other dozen passengers enjoyed his comments ("Now we are really going to crash!").

We landed and, thankfully, had a 3-1/2-hour layover to play and relax and prepare for the next flight. No problems, and the remainder of the trip was as pleasant as it could be with two very much awake and active little boys. We had a nice adventure.

In California, both boys were thrilled to see Joshua and Robin again, and meet their niece, Heidi. At the airport, Jonathon met his grandparents for the first time. I pointed out Grandma and Grandpa as we came down the escalator, and James ran to hug them. Jonathon followed, and hugged Grandma. I then said, "Give Grandpa a hug, too." Jonathon looked up, and saw two men in close proximity. One was Grandpa, and the other was a gentleman who might have been in his mid-twenties. Jonathon decided that that was the one, and hugged the man and said, "Hi, Grandpa." The man laughed kindly, we introduced Jonathon to the real Grandpa, and all was well.

Jonathon enjoyed all the family immensely, and especially took to my Aunt Becky. He had ten days of hugs and love and visits. He played with his cousins, "swam" at Laguna Beach, and took Disneyland by storm. His energy level remained high for most of the visit, but his behavior was not any more out of control than it is at home. I could fairly easily redirect him, and only had to hold him and help him regain control of himself a few (well, maybe several) times. We had a great time.

When it was time to leave, Jonathon was quite tearful. Aunt Becky gave him a teddy bear, and he clung to it. (We also had his stuffed seal with us, which is his security blanket. It goes everywhere with us. Seal, along with Raccoon—James' favorite animal—both came on the plane, and all over California.)

Jonathon was excited to get home and see the family, and the dogs, and tell everyone every detail that he could remember. Twice since our return home, Jonathon has announced that he misses Aunt Becky, and has become quite tearful. We called and talked to her, and to Grandma and Grandpa. He also requested talking to his cousin, Mikayla. He really enjoyed playing with her. The calls are sweet, and Jonathon has cried after each one. It is incredible to watch this little guy respond and attach to his extended family this way. I am amazed.

I cannot fully comprehend what is happening in my little Jonathon's heart, but I like what I am seeing.

Lori

May 11, 2002

Dear Lori,

I sure had to laugh at the visual images your trip stories conjured. It is truly amazing to see Jonathon's growth (through your eyes). I wish for this inspiration to be available to others, just as I also know many would be disheartened, as they are not seeing empathy and vulnerability and emotional availability emerge in their adopted or foster children, as you are seeing in Jonathon. A mom told me, today, that reading Dan Hughes' wonderful book had been very difficult for her, as she knew she just did not have all that Katie's "perfect mom" (in the book) had. I always have to keep the struggle in mind, as I sit with parents, as they try everything to find a real, live, feeling human being inside their child with RAD.

I suppose the young man will never forget being greeted and hugged by a strange boy who thought him a grandpa. Jonathon touches many, eh?

My best...
Michael

August 16, 2002

Dear Michael,

We are quite content with the present, and at the same time eagerly anticipating the future. Our current family, including our "little" Jonathon, is happy. Rebecca, Patrick, and Maggie are in California visiting Joshua, Robin, and baby Heidi. During their absence, Paul and I have been able to focus lots of attention on the boys. The times have been special, with both boys relishing the time alone with us. We have gone out to eat several times, and have had ample opportunities during those outings to work on character traits like thankfulness and contentment. Jonathon, when given an inch, wants twelve miles. He often orders one thing, and after it arrives decides he really wanted something else. Thus, the character lessons. Each outing, without exception, has had moments of correction and redirection. But each outing has ended on a positive note, and I think a few things have been learned. It has been a good time.

"My advice to parents considering adopting a child with RAD? RUN FOR YOUR LIFE! But then, if they took that advice, they would miss out..."

I can honestly say that, at this point, I often *enjoy* having Jonathon as my son. Long ago I loved having him, and have always wanted to have him, and we learned to truly love him, but I have only recently arrived at the point where it is a joy to watch his progress and it is a joy to be his mom.

My biggest hurdle is still the waking hour. It is vital that I get to the gym, get home, make coffee and have some quiet time to focus my attitude *before* he wakes up. (He usually wakes about 8AM.) He is still very difficult (and mean) as he awakens, and I must spend the time holding him, singing "Good Morning To You", and refocusing him. Quite honestly, I dread this time, which is why I need to get myself geared up before he rears his cute little head. I have to adjust *my* attitude before I can handle *his*.

But, other than the morning hour, the other negative episodes are usually manageable. They are, I believe, now outnumbered by happy times: times when we actually share belly laughs and smiles and hugs and just plain happiness. Jonathon loves to laugh, and there are times when we see him with his guard down, and the laughs are so genuine that we laugh until we cry.

"Hope Village" is rapidly progressing. We are currently fundraising, and brainstorming ideas to make it happen.

So we enjoy today with our family, and wonder what surprises await as the plans for Hope Village unfold. These times are truly good.

Lori

May 13, 2003

Dear Michael,

From time to time I just feel a need to share some cute Jonathonism with you, and today is one of those times!

Our young man is growing like a weed, and continues to amaze us with his emotional progress. A sense of humor is emerging, and his confidence is winning out over some of his fears. An incredible thing to watch this little person, as he changes.

Jonathon, James and I went to see "The Jonah Movie". Leaving the theater on a snowy afternoon, I was absolutely at peace as I walked hand in hand with my two youngest sons. There was the chitchat about the movie, and the popcorn, and all of the regular stuff. And then Jonathon hit me with, "Mom, I think I want to forgive G." [a former foster mother]. The discussion that followed was mind-boggling. Jonathon wanted to be sure that he could forgive someone and not have to see them to do it. He was full of questions. Full of emotion. And ready for answers. I think he began to heal some of his wounds that afternoon.

As time goes on, Jonathon seems more and more confident in our love. He tests us less frequently. He is not an angel, and misbehaves daily. But the *big* tests, the I-will-not-allow-you-into-my-heart challenges, have diminished. He is now a little boy looking for love and boundaries and security. And he is finding all of that, and *accepting* it. Just incredible.

Okay, to give you an idea about some of the "misbehaves daily" stuff: The other day I was in my craft room, scrap-booking with a friend. Jonathon and a little female friend of his were playing. I thought they were in the rec room, but I heard their voices in the laundry room. I thought that was odd, so I listened carefully. I heard Jonathon's voice, puzzled, saying, "I guess doggies whiskers don't catch on fire." I raced in there to find Jonathon holding the fireplace lighter while the little girl held Gidget's head. The horror that could have happened flashed before me! But, alas, it did not.

So today I am sitting at my computer, working on Hope Village stuff, when in walks Jonathon. He has a serious look on his face, and says he needs to talk to me. I turn to him, look him in the eyes, and ask what is on his mind. He steps closer, his eyes meeting mine, and asks a very deep question. "Mom, if I was an ant, would you still love me?" My answer, of course, is yes. I assure him that I would love him, no matter what he was. But I also say that I am very happy that he is a boy.

Michael, the part that hit me about the conversation was not his cute question, but that he knows that he is loved. "Mom, would you *still* love me?" He accepts that he is loved now, and just wondered if anything could change that.

Lori

May 13, 2003

Dear Lori,

It's hard to fathom that this could be the same boy. What a testimonial to the spirit that was alive in him, and that you were somehow able to touch. I wonder what, in "The Jonah Movie" (if anything) evoked that impulse to forgive.

My best to you all…
Michael

July 10, 2003

Good Morning, Michael,

I have been sitting here doing Hope Village work, and decided to take a quick break and give you an update on our "little" Jonathon.

It seems that Jonathon was progressing quite well, and we had not needed holding times for weeks, when I decided to accompany a friend to Korea for a week to do some adoption/orphanage work. Our little guy was clearly unsettled by my absence, even though it was discussed and he was in excellent hands while I was away. Rebecca spent lots of special time with him, and Paul was as attentive as possible. Jonathon did not erupt in huge, violent ways. He just became very sneaky, with tons of lies about anything and everything. Apparently there were lots of opportunities to hold Jonathon while I was away, and those opportunities have continued since my return home a week ago today.

When I first returned home, Jonathon's behaviors escalated, of course. I did not expect otherwise, so I was not alarmed. I became his constant companion, similar to the way it was in the early days. Then on Tuesday we reinstituted the morning routine, and that seems to have made a difference. The morning routine is to wake Jonathon up *slowly*, rubbing his back and singing gently. As he wakes, there is a long period of cuddling and talking. Then we get dressed, go downstairs for a quiet two-person breakfast, making sure other stimulants (like siblings and dogs) are not around. After a quiet breakfast, he seems ready to face life. The routine takes about an hour most days, and it is not necessary most of the time. But when Jonathon gets into a slump, it seems to be helpful in getting him back on track.

It is easy to forget how horrible the early days were, until we are faced with a smattering of the behaviors, from time to time. That is when we become very thankful that, for the most part, life is much easier for Jonathon these days.

I realize more and more, with each passing month and year, that RAD does not go away. Give Jonathon a trauma, and watch him crumble. I am thankful that Jonathon is a child who responded to the therapies and work that we could find and implement, and am aware that I will need to stay on top of my game for years to come if we want to achieve the healthiest life possible for him. I am thankful that God saw us up to this task. If we had been presented with the whole picture up front, Jonathon would have never entered our door. We would not have been willing. The work takes a toll. But the rewards are tremendous, and a changed life is appearing right before our eyes. The work is so very much worth the toll! We have learned so much, and we, ourselves, have changed for the better. None of us can grow if we are not stretched a bit.

Lori

"It was like a daily feeding that kept the hope alive, until the day came when we actually saw a glimmer of change."

July 13, 2003

Dear Lori,

It was wonderful to hear from you again. Yes, it's really true isn't it? RAD is forever, not unlike many diseases. That's not a despairing thing to say. It's just a fact. So there is triumph in good days, and there need not be shock about the bad days (unless one has forgotten about the disease). I'm amazed that this is so apparent to you. I have watched many parents sink, even after their child has made huge gains, upon their discovery that it's not "all over now". There's something about the idea that it will never be truly over that disables many parents. For you, however, it seems only to make sense, much as it is the case that a parent whose baby dies remains forever a parent whose baby died, even after the acute grieving and tears are over.

So you have the energy to resurrect the morning ritual, and you don't resent that the need for it has shown itself once again.

I do have a question, asked purely to aid me. You said: "If we had been presented with the whole picture up front, Jonathon would never have entered our door." How would you guide me in talking with prospective adoptive parents (particularly those who are fostering, and wondering about adoption) about what to expect, about how RAD often plays out? How much should I say? It goes against my grain to withhold, and it is a principle of mine that parents should give only *informed* consent. But I don't want to run people off who might find a way to do what you have done.

Thanks again for keeping me up to date.
Michael

July 21, 2003

Dear Michael,

My advice to parents considering adopting a RAD child? RUN FOR YOUR LIFE! But then, if they took that advice, they would miss out on all of the joy that we have experienced with our Jonathon. So that would actually be pretty bad advice. I believe, in many adoptions, that the primary focus is (or should be) on the needs of the child, anyway. So here is my real advice:

A parent does have the right to full disclosure. We all have different gifts and talents, and not everyone has the temperament to raise a child with RAD. The parent should be allowed the freedom to consider all aspects of the adoption before moving forward. It is in the best interests of the parents/existing family, as well as the best interests of the child with RAD. The last thing that a child with RAD needs, as you know, is a failed adoption on top of whatever they may have experienced already. Therefore, full disclosure is vital.

A parent needs to be assured that help is available. A support network should be set up before the child enters the home. Lots of reading and education should also happen before the child arrives, if possible. The parents should be told of the good stories, with happy progress. They should read, *Building the Bonds of Attachment* (Daniel Hughes, Jason Aronson, Inc., 1998), they should see your film ("Multiple Transitions: A Young Child's Point of View About Foster Care and Adoption") and read *The Jonathon Letters* (we really *should* publish these, someday) and be encouraged that these outcomes are possible. They should also be aware that these outcomes are not guaranteed, and that—even if progress is made—there will be slumps and discouraging moments. They should be taught to keep the "big picture" in sight. That will help with the daily disappointments. They should be told that there will be moments when the child will blow it, even after much progress. They should also be aware that there will be moments when *they* will blow it. We are all human, we all have limits to what we can endure, and sometimes, against our better judgment, we might act just as bad as our child with RAD.

I believe that an informed, educated parent will do a much better job with the child with RAD than one who does not fully understand how hard it will be. Much of the understanding will come easier if they try to truly grasp what the child has gone through, and why it is that he does these things. Empathy allows us to give much more of ourselves than we would have thought possible.

Once we started therapy, emails a la Michael, and reading, our lives with Jonathon had purpose and made a bit of sense. Prior to that, we were just plain frustrated and angry. This new foster child of ours was so out of control! In my heart of hearts, I wanted to beat him! I didn't, partly because it is against my parenting beliefs, and partly because it is against the foster parenting agreement. But I really wanted to! I have never had that feeling towards a child before Jonathon, and it scared me. It was all I could do to keep myself in control, which left little energy for me to work on the "hopeless" child. But once I read about RAD, and about Katy (in Hughes' book), and heard about other children, things started to fit into place. There was a diagnosis, and help available, and learning to do. Getting busy about the problem helped me, long before it actually made a difference with Jonathon. I was doing *something* about it. I was beginning to understand. I had some hope.

If no one had given me any hope in those early days, there is just no way I would have survived. My instincts said that there had to be a way, but I was so tired, and just hung on every bit of encouragement from you and Jon and the books. It was like a daily feeding that kept the hope alive, until the day came when we actually saw a glimmer of change.

As I look forward in Jonathon's life, I wonder many things. How much does Jonathon need to tell to a future wife, in order to have her aware if issues crop up that do not make sense to her? How much should a teacher know, and how much is Jonathon's private info, not to be shared? How will Jonathon react when he has his own children, and will it cause any unresolved issues to surface?

One thing I know for sure: kids will do the unexpected, twist our emotions in knots, and keep us on our toes. This is true of all kids. I often worry that parents who have not birthed children will blame all the "bad" on adoption or RAD or whatever else there is. Sometimes, kids will just decide to make bad decisions. It is just a natural part of the growing, maturing process.

Those are my thoughts on the "what to tell parents" issue.

Lori

references

Allred, D. (Fall, 1993). The dream that turned into a nightmare. *Attachments* (newsletter of the Attachment Center at Evergreen).

Axness, M. (1999). Personal communication.

Beebe, B. and Lachmann, P. (1994). Representations and internalization in infancy: Three principles of salience. *Psychoanalytic Psychology,* 11, 127–165.

Bowlby, J. (1951). *Maternal care and mental health.* Monograph Series No. 2. Geneva: World Health Organization.

Brazleton, T. and Cramer, B. (1990). *The earliest relationship: Parents, infants, and the drama of early attachment.* Reading, MA: Addison-Wesley.

Bretherton, I. (1987). New perspectives on attachment relations: Security, communication and internal working models. In J. Osofsky (Ed.) *Handbook of infant development* (Second Edition). New York: Jon Wiley and Sons, 1061–1100.

Cline, F. (1990). *Parenting with love and logic.* Colorado Springs, CO: Pinon Press.

Cline, F. (1992). *Understanding and treating the severely disturbed child.* Evergreen, CO: Evergreen Consultants in Human Behavior, EC Publications.

Federici, R. (October-December, 2000). Raising the post-institutionalized child: Risks, challenges, and innovative treatment. *The Signal* (newsletter of the World Association for Infant Mental Health), 8 (4).

Freud, A. and Burlingham, D. (1943). *War and children.* New York: Medical War Books.

Fraiberg, S.; Adelson, E. and Shapiro, V. (Summer, 1975). Ghosts in the Nursery: A Psychoanalytic approach to the problems of impaired infant-mother relationships. *Journal of the American Academy of Child Psychiatry.* 14 (3), 387–421.

Hrdy, S. (1999). *Mother nature: A history of mothers, infants and natural selection.* New York: Pantheon.

Hughes, D. (1997). *Facilitating developmental attachment: The road to emotional recovery and behavioral change in foster and adopted children.* Northvale, NJ: Jason Aronson.

Hughes, D. (1998). *Building the bonds of attachment: Awakening love in deeply troubled children.* Northvale, NJ: Jason Aronson.

James, B. (1994). *Handbook for treatment of attachment-trauma problems in children.* New York: The Free Press.

Jernberg, A. (1979). *Theraplay.* San Francisco: Jossey-Bass.

Keck, G. and Kupecky, R. (1995). *Adopting the hurt child: Hope for families with special-needs kids.* Colorado Springs, CO: Pinon Press.

Levy, T. and Orlans, M. (1998). *Attachment, trauma and healing: Understanding and treating attachment disorder in children and families.* Washington, D.C.: CWLA Press.

Lozoff, B.; Brittenham, G.; Trause, M.; Kennell, J.; and Klaus, M. (July, 1977). The mother-newborn relationship: Limits of adaptability. *The Journal of Pediatrics,* 91 (1), 1–12.

Magid, K. and McKelvey, C. (1987). *High-risk: Children without a conscience.* New York: Bantam.

Main, M.; Kaplan, N. and Cassidy, J. (1985). Security in infancy, child-
hood and adulthood: A move to the level of representation. In Bretherton,
I. And Waters, E. (Eds.). *Monographs of the Society for Research in Child
Development*, 66–103.

Provence, S. and Lipton, R. (1962). *Infants in institutions*. New York:
International Universities Press.

Randolph, L. (Spring, 1995). The neurological connection in attachment
disordered children. *Attachments* (newsletter of the Attachment Center at
Evergreen).

Rutter, M. (1970). Psychological development: Predictions from infancy.
Journal of Child Psychology and Psychiatry, 11, 49–62.

Schore, A. (2001). Minds in the making: Attachment, the self-organizing
brain, and developmentally-oriented psychoanalytic psychotherapy. *British
Journal of Psychotherapy*, 17 (3).

Schore, A. (2002). Dysregulation of the right brain: A fundamental mech-
anism of traumatic attachment and the psychopathogenesis of posttrau-
matic stress disorder. *Australian and New Zealand Journal of Psychiatry*, 36
(1).

Siegel, D. (1995). Memory, trauma and psychotherapy: A cognitive sci-
ence view. *Journal of Psychotherapy Practice and Research*, 4, 93–112.

Siegel, D. (1999). *The developing mind: Toward a neurobiology of interpersonal experience*. New York: The Guilford Press.

Spitz, R. (1945). Hospitalism: An inquiry into the genesis of psychiatric
conditions in early childhood. *Psychoanalytic Study of the Child*, 1, 53–74.

Stern, D. (1985). *The interpersonal world of the human infant*. New York:
Basic Books.

Stern, D. (1995). *The motherhood constellation*. New York: Basic Books.

Thomas, N. (1997). *When love is not enough: A guide to parenting children with RAD.* (Available from the author at Families by Design, Box 2812, Glenwood Springs, CO 81602.

Trout, M. (1982). The language of parent-infant interaction: A tool in the assessment of jeopardized attachments in infancy. In J. Stack (Ed.), *The special infant.* New York: Human Sciences Press.

Welch, M. (1988). *Holding Time.* New York: Simon and Schuster.

White, B. (Winter, 1997). Depression and parenting a child with attachment difficulties. *Attachments* (Newsletter of The Attachment Center at Evergreen), pp. 1–2.

Winnicott, D. (1975). *From paedetriatics to psycho-analysis.* New York: Basic Books.

Yarrow, L. (1967). The development of focused relationships in infancy. In J. Hellmuth (Ed.). *Exceptional infant.* New York: Bruner/Mazel, 492–442.

resources

FILMS

Episode of "48 Hours", April 6, 1995: "Afraid of Our Children". Available from CBS Video.

Trout, M. (1997). "Multiple Transitions: A Young Child's Point of View on Foster Care and Adoption". 16-minute videotape, available from The Infant-Parent Institute, 328 North Neil, Champaign, IL 61820 USA; tel: 217-352-4060; email: mtrout@infant-parent.com; website: www.infant-parent.com

Trout, M. (2004). "IS ANYONE IN THERE? Adopting a Wounded Child" 13-minute video, available in DVD or VHS format from The Infant-Parent Institute, 328 North Neil, Champaign, IL 61820 USA; tel: 217-352-4060; email: mtrout@infant-parent.com; website: www.infant-parent.com

NEWSLETTERS/ORGANIZATIONS

ATTACh, An Association for Treatment and Training in the Attachment of Children, Box 879, Evergreen, CO 80439.

Attachment Disorder Parents Network, Box 18475, Boulder, CO 80308.

Attachment disorder website: http://attachmentdisorder.net.

The Institute for Attachment and Child Development (formerly the Attachment Center at Evergreen, Colorado), Box 730, Kittredge, CO 80457; website: http://www.instituteforattachment.org.

The Parent Network for the Post-Institutionalized Child, Box 163, Meadow Lands, PA 15347.

World Association for Infant Mental Health, c/o University Outreach and Engagement, Michigan State University, Kellogg Center, Garden Level, East Lansing, MI 48824.

OTHER READINGS

Gottman, J. and Declaire, J. (1998). *Raising an emotionally intelligent child.* New York: Simon and Schuster.

Perry, B.; Pollard, R.; Blakley, T.; Baker, W. and Vigilante, D. (Winter, 1995,). Childhood trauma, the neurobiology of adaptation, and "use-dependent" development of the brain: How "states" become "traits". *Infant Mental Health Journal,* 16 (4), 271–289.

Van der kolk, B. and McFarlane, A. (1996). The black hold of trauma. In van der kolk, B; McFarlane, A. and Weisaeth, L. (Eds.). *Traumatic stress: The effects of overwhelming experience on mind, body, society.* New York: The Guilford Press.

Verny, T. (2002). *Tomorrow's baby.* New York: Simon and Schuster.

Yehuda, R.; Halligan, S. and Grossman, R. (2001). Childhood trauma and risk for PTSD: Relationship to intergenerational effects of trauma, parental PTSD, and cortisol. *Development and Psychopathology,* 13, 733–753.